1,000,000 Books

are available to read at

www.ForgottenBooks.com

Read online
Download PDF
Purchase in print

ISBN 978-0-259-37585-2
PIBN 10814642

1 MONTH OF
FREE
READING

at

www.ForgottenBooks.com

By purchasing this book you are eligible for one month membership to ForgottenBooks.com, giving you unlimited access to our entire collection of over 1,000,000 titles via our web site and mobile apps.

To claim your free month visit: www.forgottenbooks.com/free814642

English
Français
Deutsche
Italiano
Español
Português

www.forgottenbooks.com

Mythology Photography **Fiction**
Fishing Christianity **Art** Cooking
Essays Buddhism Freemasonry
Medicine **Biology** Music **Ancient**
Egypt Evolution Carpentry Physics
Dance Geology **Mathematics** Fitness
Shakespeare **Folklore** Yoga Marketing
Confidence Immortality Biographies
Poetry **Psychology** Witchcraft
Electronics Chemistry History **Law**
Accounting **Philosophy** Anthropology
Alchemy Drama Quantum Mechanics
Atheism Sexual Health **Ancient History**
Entrepreneurship Languages Sport
Paleontology Needlework Islam
Metaphysics Investment Archaeology
Parenting Statistics Criminology
Motivational

A

NEW VERSION

OF THE

P S A L M S

OF

D A V I D.

By the Reverend THOMAS CRADOCK, Rector of
St. Thomas's, Baltimore County, MARYLAND.

ANNAPOLIS:
Printed by JONAS GREEN, MDCCLVI.

To His EXCELLENCY

HORATIO SHARPE, Eſq;

Governor of the Province of *MARYLAND,*

AND

To the HONOURABLE

JAMES HAMILTON, Eſq;

Late Governor of the Province of *PENNSYLVANIA,*

This New VERSION of the
PSALMS of *DAVID,* is,
with all Humility and grateful Acknowledgment,

DEDICATED,

BY

Their moſt obliged,

Humble Servant,

Thomas Cradock.

THE *Author of the following* VERSION *owns himself under the higheſt* Obligation *to his kind and generous Subſcri- bers ; and modeſtly hopes, that, if they cannot applaud, they will, at leaſt, excuſe his Preſumption, in attempting ſo bold and difficult a* Work. *He is ſorry, that he could not comply with his Propoſals as to the Time ; but he was twice diſappointed of his Paper, and then thought it moſt expedient to wait a little longer for the Advantage of new Types.*

SUBSCRIBERS.

HIS Excellency HORATIO SHARPE, Efq; Governor of *Maryland.*

The Honourable JAMES HAMILTON, Efq; late Governor of *Pennfylvania,*   18 Books.

A

MR. Robert Adair, 2
Rev. Mr. Francis Allifon,
  of *Philadelphia,* 6
Dr. Ephraim Andrews.
Mr. George Afhman.

B

Rev. Mr. Thomas Bacon, 6
Mr. Alexander Beall.
Mr. William Beafman.
Capt. John Bond.
Mr. John Bond.
Mr. Richard Bond.
Mr. Thomas Bond.
Capt. Zachariah Bond.
Mrs. Sarah Boone.
Mr. Beale Bordley.
Stephen Bordley, Efq; 4
Mr. Stephen Bordley, junr. 2
Mr. Roger Boyce, 2
Mr. William Bradford.
Mr. John Brafhear.
Mr. Hubbard Brewen.
John Brice, Efq; 6

Rev. Mr. William Brogden, 2
Rev. Mr. Clement Brooke, of
  New-Caftle.
Rev. Mr. Richard Browne.
Mr. Lloyd Buchanan, 4

C

Hon. Benjamin Calvert, Efq; 6
Rev. Mr. Ifaac Campbell, 2
Mr. William Carmichael.
Mr. Chriftopher Carnan, 6
Mr. John Carnan, 2
Mr. Rowland Carnan, 2
Charles Carroll, Efq; 6
Dr. Charles Carroll, 4
Mr. James Cary, 2
Mr. Daniel Chamier.
Mr. Samuel Chapman.
Mr. Jeremiah Chafe.
Mr. Richard Chafe.
Rev. Mr. Thomas Chafe.
Mr. Arthur Chenworth.
Charles Chriftie, Efq; 2
Mr. James Chriftie, 2
Mr. Thomas Cockey.
Mr. John Cooke.

Mr.

Mr. John Cornelius.

Mr. John Cromwell, 2

Mr. Joseph Cromwell.

Mr. Charles Croxall, 2

Mr. Richard Croxall, 2

Mr William Cummins.

D

Mr. William Dallam, 2

Henry Darnall, Esq; 4

Mr. John Darnall, 3

Mr. John Day.

Rev. Mr. Hugh Deans, 10

Mr. Benjamin Deaver.

William Denune, M. D.

Mr. Ignatius Digges, 2

Capt. James Dobbins, 3

Edward Dorfey, Esq; 4

Mr. John Hammond Dorfey, 2

Mr. Joshua Dorfey, 2

Mr. Nicholas Dorfey.

Daniel Dulany, Esq; 2

Daniel Dulany, junr. Esq; 2

Capt. Dennis Dulany, 3

Walter Dulany, Esq; 6

Mr. John Duvall.

E

Mr. John Eden.

Capt. James Edmondson.

Mr. John Enfor, junior, 2

F

Benjamin Franklin, Esq; of
    Philadelphia, 12

Mr. Thomas Franklin.

G

Capt. Nicholas Ruxton Gay, 2

Mr. John Gill.

Mr. Christopher Gist.

Mrs. Susanna Gist.

Mr. Thomas Gist.

Mr. William Gist.

Mr. Peter Gosnell.

Mrs. Lovelefs Gossuch.

Mr. William Govane, 4

Capt. Henry Griffith.

Mr. Luke Griffith.

H

Mr. Acquilla Hall.

Col. John Hall, 2

Mr. John Hall, 2

Mr. John Hall, of *Cranbury,* 3

Mr. Joshua Hall, 3

Alexander Hamilton, M. D. 2

Mr. William Hamilton.

Mr. William Hanson, junr.

Rev. Mr. Richard Harrison.

Mr. Thomas Harrison, 2

Mr. John Hawkins.

Mr. Mayberry Helms.

Mr. Andrew Heugh.

Mr. Robert Horner.

Mr. Cornelius Howard.

Capt. Michael Hubbert, 2

Col. John Hunter, of *Virginia,* 2

Mr. John Hurd.

I

Hon. Edmund Jenings, Esq;

Dr. John Jackson.

Mr. Lancelot Jacques,

Mr. James Johnson.

Mr. Thomas Johnson.

Mr. Philip Jones,

Mr. Thomas Jones.

Mr. James Jordan.

Mr. William Jordan.

Mr. Angelo Israelo.

Mr.

K

Mr. Hopewell Keene.
Mr. James Kelley.
Mr. William Kelley.
Philip Key, Esq;   4

L

Rev. Mr. Charles Lake.
Mr. Thomas Lancaster.
Mr. Alexander Lawson,   12
Rev. Mr. Andrew Lendrum,   2
Mr. Stead Lowe.
Mr. William Lux, of *Annapolis*,   2
Mr. William Lux, of *Baltimore*,   6
Dr. William Lyon,   4

M

Mr. Nicholas Maccubbin,   2
Michael Macnemarra, Esq;
Mr. Nathan Magruder.
Mr. John Matthews.
Mr. George Maxwell.
Mrs. Elizabeth McLeod,   3
Mr. Anthony M'Culloch,   3
Mr. David M'Culloch,   3
Mr. James McLachlan.
Rev. Mr. John MacPherson,   2
Mr. John Metcalfe.
Mr. John Moale,   2
Mr. John Moffatt,   3
Rev. Mr. John Moncure, of *Virginia*.
Thomas Moore, Esq; of *Antigua*,   3
Mr. William Murdock.
Mr. Joseph Murray.
Rev. Mr. John Myers,   2

N

Mr. Edward Neale.
Mr. John Needham,   3

Mr. Benjamin Norris,   2
Mr. Thomas Norris.
Capt. Benjamin North,   2
Mrs. Catharine North,   2

O

Mr. George Ogg, junr.
Mr. Stephen Onion.
Mr. John Orrick.
Mr. Nicholas Orrick.
Mrs. Susanna Orrick.
Mrs. Elizabeth Owings.
Mr. Joshua Owings,   2
Mrs. Mary Owings.
Mr. Samuel Owings,   2
Mr. Stephen Heart Owings.

P

Mr. John Paca,   4
Mr. John Paca, junr.   2
Mr. Robert Patterson.
Rev. Mr. Richard Peters, of *Philadelphia*,   6
Mr. James Phillips,   2
Mr. Brian Philpot, junr.   4
Mr. John Pindell.
Mr. William Potts,   3
Mr. George Presbury,   2
Mr. Edward Punteney.

R

John Raitt, Esq;
Mr. Christopher Randall.
Mr. Christopher Randall, junr.
Mr. William Reynolds.
Mr. James Richard,   2
Capt. Joseph Richardson,   2
Major Charles Ridgely,   10
Mr. John Risteau,   2
Mr. Talbot Risteau,   4
Mr. Nicholas Rogers,   2

Mr.

SUBSCRIBERS.

Mr William Rogers.
Dr. David Rofs, 6
John Rofs, Efq;

S

Rev. Mr. James Scott, of *Virginia*.
Mr. John Shelmordine.
Mr. Thomas Sheredine, 2
Mr. John Simkins.
Mr. Thomas Sligh, 2
Mr. Samuel Soumain, of *Philadelphia*.
Mr. Thomas Sprigg.
Mr. Tobias Stanfbury, 2
Mr. Richard Stephenfon.
George Steuart, Efq; 6
Dr. John Stevenfon, 6
Mr. John Stinchcomb.
Mr. Robert Stokes.
Mr. Robert Swan, 2
Rev. Mr. Theophilus Swift, 2

T

Hon. Benjamin Tafker, Efq; 17
Hon. Benj. Tafker, junr. Efq;
Rev. Mr. Mofes Tabbs.
Mr. John Thomas.
Mr. Dowdall Thompfon.
Rev. Mr. Thomas Thornton, 4

Mr. William Thornton.
Mr. James Tilghman.
Col. Richard Tilghman.
Capt. Walter Tolley, 2

W

Dr. Edward Wakeman, 4
Dr. James Walker, 3
Mr. Charles Wallace.
Mr. James Wardrop, 6
Mr. John Wardrop, 4
Mr. Godfrey Waters, 2
Mr. Nicholas Watkins.
Mr. John Webfter.
Mr. John Welfh.
Mr. Alexander Wells.
Mr. Charles Wells.
Mr. Thomas Wells.
Mr. Stephen Weft, 6
Col. Thomas White, 3
Mr. John Willmott.
Mr. Richard Willmott, 2
Mr. Daniel Wolftenholme, 2

Y

Hon. Benjamin Young, Efq; 6
Benjamin Young, junr. Efq; 3
Mr. Samuel Young.
Col. William Young, 2

THE PSALMS OF DAVID.

PSALM I.

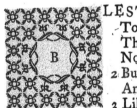

BLEST is the man, whose honeſt ſoul diſdains
‑To tread the path where impious counſel reigns,
That in the way of ſinners has not ſtood,
Nor fill'd the chair of the imperious proud.
2 But makes *Jehovah*'s law his dear delight,　5
And meditates thereon by day, by night.
3 Like ſome fair tree, that near a riv'let grows,
　And ſhades the waters with it's ſpreading
Boughs, that nor wither, nor deluſive are,　　　[boughs,
But with their fruit reward the planter's care,　　10
He'll flouriſh long ---- of heav'n itſelf the love,
And ev'ry ſolid joy and comfort prove.
4 Not ſo the wicked ---- like the chaff that flies,
　And ſcatters far, when driving winds ariſe;
　By the black whirlwind of their paſſions tóſt,　　15
　In guilt, and in it's direful woes they 're loſt.
5 When therefore at the laſt tremendous day
　Comes forth th' almighty judge in dread array;

B

Struck

Struck with their crimes, his presence shall they fly,
Nor join the righteous in their songs of joy.   20
6 For well our God the just man's way discerns,
   That he the path to heav'n with rapture learns;
   While impious men, who tread of sin the road,
 ·For ever perish-----such thy will, O God!

P S A L M II.

1 WHAT desp'rate madness strikes the heathen? Say,
        What vain delusive hopes the nations sway?
2 Earth's haughty tyrants in their pride rebel;
   With impious rage the mad'ning rulers swell;
 · Thro' all, thro' all, the fatal frenzy flies;   5
   Against the Lord, against his Christ, they rise.
3 " Our souls (they boast) we'll from this bondage free,
   " And vindicate our native liberty."
4 But they in vain Omnipotence defy,
   The great, the sov'reign Lord, that rules on high,   10
   Laughs all their empty menaces to scorn;
5 See, see against them his dread fury burn!
   Hear 'gainst his enemies his thunder break!
   Hear him (O hear) the solemn mandate speak;
6 " Thou still, my son, on sacred *Sion* reign,   15
   " And o'er the conquer'd globe my pow'r maintain."
7 For me, while breath inspires this vital frame,
   The law my God hath giv'n me, I'll proclaim;
   " This day, my son, have I begotten thee;
8 " Ask of thy sov'reign father-----thine shall be   20
   " Whate'er the regions of the world contain,
   " Whatever *æther* bounds, whate'er the main;
9 " Thou with an iron rod the nations sway;
   " Bruise them, like vessels form'd of potter's clay."
10 But hear, ye monarchs of the world, be wise;   25
    Dispel this dark'ning mist before your Eyes;
11 Serve the great father, and his will revere;
    Temper your joy with pure, with holy fear,
12 Embrace the Son, and due obedience shew;
    If but awhile his dire resentment glow,   30
    Eternal death's your doom-----thrice happy all,
    Who trust in him, on his dread name who call!

P S A L M

P S A L M III.

1 HOW 'num'rous, Lord, how ſtrong, how powerful they,
  Who riſe againſt me, and my ſoul diſmay ?
2 Vain, empty boaſters ! In their guilt they're proud,
  And, that my God diſdains me, vaunt aloud.
3 But me thro' dangers haſt thou ſafely led,
  And crown'd with glory and ſucceſs my head ;   5
4 On thee I call'd in confidence of pray'r,
  And from thy ſacred hill thou deign'dſt to hear.
5 At Night I laid me down, and ſlept ſecure ;
  At Morn I roſe, ſupported by thy pow'r.   10
6 Why then, tho' thouſands threat me, ſhou'd I fear ?
  My ſhield thy goodneſs, I defy the ſpear.
7 Riſe, Lord, aſſiſt me-----ſave me from my Foes ;
  Long has thy dreadful wrath againſt them roſe ;
  My only Foes the abandon'd wicked are,   15
  And oft th' inflictions of thy hand they bear :
8 While all thy bleſſings righteous ſouls attend,
  And them thou'lt ſave, who in thy temple bend.

P S A L M IV.

1 ALL-CLEMENT God, that know'ſt my honeſt Mind ;
  In thee from ill a ſure relief I find ;
  Oft in my ſad diſtreſs, thou'ſt giv'n releaſe ;
  Again my ſoul implores her wonted peace ;
  Benign, O liſten to thy ſervant's pray'r ;   5
  Have mercy on me, Lord, in pity ſpare.
2 Ye hapleſs ſons of men, what frenzy ſways ?
  How long 'gainſt me your calumnies you'll raiſe ?
  How long indulge your vile malignant ſpite ?
  How long in killing ſlanders take delight ?   10
3 To your confuſion know, the Godhead loves
  The man, who by his works his duty proves ;
  Nor, when in humble guiſe I to him plain,
  Shall his obedient ſervant plead in vain.
4 Stand then, ye wretches, of his pow'r in awe ;   15
  Nor ſin preſumptuous 'gainſt his ſacred law ;
  Reflect your actions in the ſilent night-----
  Your hearts will own you guilty in his ſight.
6 The heedleſs *many* in vain riches truſt,
  And hope, their pray'rs for opulence, are juſt :   20
  But I more happy, if thy light divine
  On my glad ſoul in it's full radiance ſhine ;

        More

7 More happy, thou, my only joy and hope,
  Than when the nectar fparkles in my cup;
  Than when with corn my granaries abound,
  And loaded olives croud the fertile ground.   25

8 Yes, my good God, I'll lay me down in peace;
  I'll fleep, devoid of care, fecure of eafe;
  Thou, only thou, canft diffipate my grief,
  From foes give fafety, and from pain relief.   30

P S A L M *V.*

1 ALL-POW'RFUL Lord, thy fuppliant fervant hear;
    Thou art my God; to thee I fly in pray'r;
  Thou art my King; thou in my heart doft reign;
  Ah! not thy *David's* humble fuit difdain.

3 At early dawn my faithful voice I'll raife;   5
  At early dawn I'll fupplicate thy grace.

4 No pleafure tak'ft thou in impiety,
  Nor wilt thou fuffer fin to dwell with thee.

5 The fool, that hears not thy commands with awe;
  The foul deprav'd, that deviates from thy law,   10
  The impious tongue, that deals in fraudful lies;
  The hand, it's maker's image that deftroys,
  Are hateful to thee all, and foon fhall know
  The direful pains thy vengeance dooms them to.

7 But on thy mercy fhall my foul rely;   15
  When I with rev'rence to thy temple fly,
  When at thy altar I devoutly kneel,
  Bleft with thy light, what awful joy I feel?

8 Direct me, O my God, the fnares t' evade,
  Which my relentlefs enemies have laid,   20

9 Deceit and wrong their boaft, fair truth their fcorn,
  Their villain-hearts with horrid mifchiefs burn,
  More black their throats than the remorfelefs grave,
  And with their tongues they flatter, to deceive.

10 Do thou, O God, the impious race deftroy;   25
  Thro' their own wild devices let them die;
  'Gainft thee they dare rebel;-----affert thy pow'r,
  And bear their vile atrocious crimes no more.

11 But let all they, that truft in thee, rejoice,
  And tune in hymns of gratitude their voice;   30
  In thee the greateft happinefs they prove,
  Thy will their law, thy glorious name their love.

12 For to thy will who bear a juft regard,
  Shall from thy bounty meet a full reward;

Them,

Them, who to thy commands due rev'rence have,   35
Thy gracious goodnefs, as a fhield, fhall fave.

P S A L M *VI.*

1 WHILE lafts thy dread refentment! Lord, forbear;
   Difpleas'd, thy chaftifements are too fevere.
2 Have mercy, Lord-----a languid weaknefs reigns;
   Heal my diftemper'd bones, and eafe my pains.
3 Inceffant ills my anguifh'd foul diftrefs;   5
   How long wilt thou delay, till thou redrefs?
4 Still I'll implore thee----turn, dread father, turn,
   Nor let thy mercy leave me thus forlorn.
5 In death of thee we no remembrance have,
   And who can praife thee in the filent grave?   10
6 Heaves my fad breaft the live-long night with fighs;
   Suffus'd with conftant ftreams my fleeplefs eyes;
   My bed I water with the briny flood;
   Swims my wet couch with tears, O pitying God;
7 No more with florid Health my vifage glows;   15
   The lilly now looks pale; where blufh'd the rofe;
   My fight's impair'd, my body wears away,
   While cruel foes hafte on the fwift decay!
8 Far hence, ye impious crouds; the Lord hath heard
   My earneft pray'r, my anguifh'd foul he 'as chear'd;   20
9 My earneft pray'r I've not preferr'd in vain;
   My earneft pray'r my God will not difdain.
10 Confufion fhall be theirs, that vex my foul;
   Their caufelefs enmity fhall meet controul;
   With fudden terror feiz'd, lo! back they turn,   25
   No more I'm harraft, and no more I mourn.

P S A L M *VII.*

1 O LORD my God, whom my defence I've made,
   When perfecuting foes my life invade,
   'Gainft their infidious fchemes that life defend,
   And in the threat'ning danger ftand my friend.
2 For like the favage monarch of the wood,   5
   Whofe fport is flaughter, and whofe thirft is blood,
   If thou not aidft me with thy faving pow'r,
   Their cruel jaws thy fervant will devour.
3 And yet, O Lord, if I've th' offender been,
   If I've not kept my hands from rapine clean;   10

If,

4 If, when my friend my int'reft has purfued,.
   I've paid his friendfhip with ingratitude ;
   (But fure a nobler way I always chofe,
   And oft from ruin have redeem'd my foes)

5 'Gainft me let my fierce enemy fucceed,   15
   Down in the earth my mangled carcafe tread,
   Be on the vile *ingrate*, feverely juft,
   And lay my tarnifh'd honours in the duft.

6 But thou, O Lord, in thy dread anger rife ;
   O not my humble, ardent fuit, defpife ;   20
   In all thy awful majefty array'd,
   Call forth thy vengeance to thy fervant's aid.

7 So fhall the people tremble at thy pow'r,
   And thee their king, and thee their God, adore.

8 O thou, the fov'reign judge of all mankind,   25
   Let me, as I am guiltlefs, mercy find,
   Let my integrity thy pity move ;

9 While my remorfelefs foes thy juftice prove ;
   Thou trieft the reins, the heart-----thy fearching eye
   The foul's moft fecret purpofe can defcry.   30

10 But why their bitter enmity I fear,
   When fafely guarded by th' almighty's care ;
   That gracious being that defends the good,
   And pours deftruction on the impious proud ?

12 If ftill perverfely they refift his word,   35
   Lo ! the all-high draws his avenging fword !
   See ! his bow ready bent, his arrows fly ;
   The wounded finners feel his wrath, and die.

14 Such the refult of wickednefs like theirs !
   With fin they travail, and they bring forth tears ;   40
   Big with delufive hopes of mighty gains,-----
   Death's the reward of their accurfed pains.

15 For me they made a pit-----in vain they made ;
   To the fame pit they are themfelves betray'd ;

16 On their own heads their threat'ned mifchiefs fall ;   45
   In their own fnares involv'd, they perifh all.

17 Therefore to heav'n's high Lord, in fongs of praife,
   Freed from their toils, my tuneful voice I'll raife ;
   The juft, the righteous God I'll, grateful, fing,
   And ever hymn the univerfal king.   50

          P S A L M *VIII.*

1 **O** DREAD Jehovah ! glorious is thy name ;
     According worlds it's excellence proclaim ;

                                              The

The glitt'ring regions of the spangled sky
Declare thy greatness and thy majesty.
2 How vast thy kindness to the sons of men,　　　5
E'en in our helpless infancy is seen;
If such o'er sucklings thy paternal care,
The wicked sure their blasphemies may spare.
3 But when thy wond'rous works above I spy,
The glorious canopy that hangs on high,　　　10
Rejoicing in his strength, the radiant sun,
With her attendant orbs, the glimm'ring moon;
4 Who can the depth of all thy goodness scan,
Thy free, thy vast benificence to man?
That we, mere *things* of earth, thy care can boast,　　　15
In joy, in rapt'rous wonder, I am lost.
5 With glory crown'd, ours is the second place
To the high order of th' angelic race;
6 Lord of this lower world, a wide domain,
O'er all the creatures of thy hand we reign;　　　20
7 The lowing herds, the bleating flocks obey,
And all the beasts that in the woodlands stray;
8 Ours are the wing'd inhabitants above;
The tribes are ours that in old ocean rove:
9 O dread Jehovah, glorious is thy name:　　　25
According worlds it's excellence proclaim.

P S A L M IX.

1 WITH heart sincere, thy praise, O Lord, I'll sing;
Thy wond'rous works extol, my God, my king:
2 By thee supported, I'll in thee rejoice;
Thy name, thy praise, thy pow'r, shall fill my voice.
3 Elate in vain, my vanquish'd foes are fled;　　　5
They perish; lo! thy presence strikes them dead:
4 For thou my righteous cause hast made *thy own*,
And spoke thy judgments from thy awful throne:
5 Thou bad'st the *heathen* give their madness o'er;
By thee their names eras'd, shall live no more.　　　10
6 Imperious foe; thy menaces are void,
Like the sack'd cities, by thy rage destroy'd.
7 But thou, O mighty Lord, shalt ever reign,
Thy just tribunal ever shalt maintain;
8 By righteous acts thy faithful people sway,　　　15
And shield the pious souls who thee obey.
9 A certain refuge to the sore-opprest,
Thou, when thy wisdom wills, shalt give them rest.

Thee

10 Thee her support the anguish'd soul shall make,
   Assur'd, thy servants thou wilt, ne'er forsake.   20
11 Ye sons of *Sion*, his high name extol;
   Shout forth his praises to the nations all;
12 Not unreveng'd he lets the guiltless die,
   And, when the humble plains, he hears his cry.
13 O gracious God, whom my defence I found,   25
   When impious foes breath'd forth destruction round,
   Preserve me still, that I in grateful lays,
   'Midst *Salem's* joyous throngs, may hymn thy praise.
15 Fall'n in the pit, for others they prepare,
   Entangled in their toils, the *heathen* are: 30
16 O wond'rous justice of a righteous God!
   From their own wily acts their ruin flow'd.
17 Thus their own schemes their own destruction prove;
   Thus perish they, who not their Maker love.
18 But all, who humbly on their God rely,   35
   Want not his aid, when in distress they cry.
19 Yes, Lord, arise-----let not vain man prevail;
   Convince them, that thy truth will never fail;
20 Make them thy sov'reign pow'r, thy justice own;
   That they're but men, that thou art God alone.   40

P S A L M X.

1 O GRACIOUS God, why standest thou afar?
   Why not thy poor afflicted servant hear?
2 The impious *atheist* persecutes the just;
   His own insidious arts he makes his trust:
   Shall he his vile insidious arts enjoy,   5
   And wilt not thou the villain brood destroy?
3 See, how he glories in his wild desires,
   And loves the man whom vain ambition fires:
4 Big with his hopes, with high presumption fraught,
   Thee he denies, thou art not in his thought!   10
5 Secure in fancied happiness he lives;
   To thy dread vengeance bold defiance gives;
   With haughty scorn looks wrathful on his foes,
   And madly bids them all his schemes oppose.
6 " Your efforts all, (he proudly cries) are vain;   15
   " To life's last verge my pow'r I will maintain,
   " No care, no anguish, shall corrode my breast;
   " No pain, no sickness, shall destroy my rest;
   " In all the blessings of this earth I'll flow,
   " And brave the highest vengeance of the foe."   20
                                                          From

7 From his vile mouth continual curfes fly;
  He fmiles at perjury, adores a lie,
  Thinks it his higheft honour, to deceive,
  And is in rapture, when the righteous grieve.

8 In the dark corners of the ftreet he lies,   25
  With wond'rous fkill prepares his treacheries,
  T' entrap the good, he fpends the live-long night;
  The good, the conftant objects of his fpite.

9 As fkulks the lion in his den, and waits,
  Till in his jaws fome heedlefs beaft he gets;   30
  So crouches he, fo lurks in ambufcade,
  The blood of helplefs innocence to fhed;
  With what malignant joy the traitor fmiles,
  When once they're hamper'd in his wily toils?

11 All this he does, and blafphemoufly proud,   35
  That thou regard'ft him not, exults aloud;
  Boafts, thou his impious projects wilt not fee;
  That *right* and *wrong* are all the fame to thee.

12 Arife, O God, lift thy avenging hand,
  Nor let the poor in vain thy aid demand,   40

13 Why fhou'd the wicked thus thy wrath defpife?
  Thou careft not for man, prophane he cries.

14 Sure thou haft heard his boaft, and feen his rage;
  The good man's caufe thy juftice will engage;
  To thee the humble plead for fwift redrefs;   45
  Implore thy mercy in their deep diftrefs;
  Own thy omnipotence, thy right divine,
  And that to punifh wickednefs is thine.

15 Break then his arm, O Lord, confound his pow'r;
  Deftroy his fchemes, that he may rage no more;   50
  Make all his vile imaginations vain,
  Nor let his crimes difturb our peace again.

16 Then fhalt thou have o'er all eternal fway;
  With humble awe thy people fhall obey;
  The madnefs of the *heathen* then fhall ceafe,   55
  And all thy righteous fervants dwell in peace.

17 Thus of the injur'd poor, the pious pray'r,
  All-clement God, thou condefcend'ft to hear;
  To thee they weep, to thee they cry, amain,
  Nor are their pious pray'rs addreft in vain: 60

18 That of th' afflicted thou affert the right
  Againft th' injuftice of the man of might;
  That he, abas'd his pride, controul'd his pow'r,
  May be the fcourge of innocence no more.

C   P S A L M

P S A L M *XI.*

1   ON the Lord with confidence rely ;
    (Sure is the aid of the divinity).
  Why then d'ye bid my foul diftruft his pow'r,
  And a vain refuge in the hills explore ;
  Like tim'rous birds, whofe flight betrays their fear,   5
  Who fwiftly fkim the fkies, when danger's near ?

2 For lo ! th' ungodly bend their hoftile bow ;
  Their arrows ready on the ftring they fhew ;
  With private fpite they at the righteous aim,
  The man, whofe confcious heart is free from blame.   10

3 But thou'lt, almighty Lord, their fury ftay ;
  The righteous thou'lt protect, who thee obey ;
  Thou wilt their helplefs innocence defend ;
  The bow with fruitlefs aim th' ungodly bend.

4 Thou in thy hallow'd temple fit'ft on high ;   15
  High in thy heav'ns, enthron'd in majefty,
  Full in thy view the fcatter'd nations are ;
  Howe'er difpers'd, they all employ thy care.

5 Thine eye the actions of the *good man* views,
  The *bad* thro' all his mazy crimes purfues ;   20
  The *good* are conftant objects of thy love ;
  The *bad* thy bitt'reft indignation prove.

6 Thou on the *bad* doft dire deftruction pour,
  Hear ! the black tempefts all around them roar,
  Hark ! the loud thunder rattles o'er their heads ;   25
  Lo ! it's fwift fires the fulph'rous lightning fheds.

7 But, juft thyfelf, thou call'ft the juft man thine,
  And bidft thy mercy on the upright fhine.

P S A L M *XII.*

1   LORD, affift ; for faith, for honour's flown ;
    Our Earth they've left, and fure to Heav'n are gone :

2 Now each man to delude his neighbour tries ;
  Their tongues are tipt with flatteries and lies.

3 But the proud tongue, that fpeaks a haughty lie,   5
  The falfe, the flattering lip, wilt thou deftroy :

4 Who fearlefs fay ; " Our lips are fure our own ;
  " Be by our perjur'd tongues our courage known ;
  " Our villain-fchemes undaunted we'll maintain ;
  " And who our tongues fhall curb, our lips fhall rein ?"   10

5 But thou fhalt hear th' afflicted's carneft fighs ;
  Thou in behalf of innocence fhalt rife ;

                                     Shalt

Shalt free their fouls from each infidious fnare,
And heal their forrows with a father's care.

6 For in thy word,. O Lord, we reft fecure,   15
Thy word, than pureft filver far more pure;
Than filver fev'n times by the fire refin'd,
It's drofs exhal'd, and fcatter'd by the wind.

7 Yes; what thy honour fpeaks, wilt thou maintain;
Their righteous fouls in all their griefs fuftain;   20
From this degen'rate race wilt fet them free,
And blefs them with their native liberty.

8 " But when unjuft and impious men bear fway,
" Then vice exults, and walks in open day."

P S A L M *XIII.*

1   HOW long wilt thou my troubled foul negleft,
Nor to my fervent pray'r have due refpeft?
How long, my God, thy prefence ftill conceal,
While I unutterable anguifh feel?
How long thus bootlefs fhall I yet complain,   5
While fneer my cruel foes, and mock my pain?

3 O hear, while I thy ftrength'ning light implore;
O hear, or foon thy fervant is no more;
Death foon on all my glories cafts a fhade,
And foon fhail I be number'd with the dead.   10

4 Then will my foes triumphant raife their voice,
And with their wonted infolence rejoice.

5 But ftill I'll place my confidence in thee;
My only joy, thy faving hand fhall be;

6 By thy bleft goodnefs rais'd, thy praife I'll fing,   15
And hymn thy glorious name, eternal king.

P S A L M · *XIV.*

1   THE impious *atheift*, in his folly proud,
At one all-powerful *being* laughs aloud.
Corrupt they're all; from virtue's path they turn,
And in the quenchlefs fires of luft they burn;
Their fhocking crimes, their curft impieties,   5
Demand tremendous vengeance from the fkies.

2 Th' All-high looks down from his etherial throne,
To fee, if man his fov'reign pow'r will own;
If yet the fons of earth accept his fway,
His name revere, and his dread will obey.   10

Ah

3 Ah no ! not one-----they 'gainſt their God conſpire,
Purſue the dictates of each wild deſire,
In filthy ſcenes their precious hours employ,
And make their ſhocking crimes their horrid joy.

4 Does then rank frenzy o'er the wicked reign,   15
That they ſuch hideous blaſphemy maintain,
That they my people, as their prey, devour,
And, obſtinate, reject almighty pow'r ?

5 But ſtill their wretched hearts ſhall ſhake with fear,
For, where the righteous are, God's always near,   20
The refuge of the juſt he'll conſtant prove ;
The humble ſoul is ſure to have his love ;

6 And, while, ye wicked, you her hopes deride,
Falls direful vengeance on your impious pride.

7 From *Sion*'s hill, O that the Lord wou'd ſend   25
His ſpeedy aid, and *Jacob*'s ſons defend ;
Wou'd his own people from their bondage free,
And give them back their long'd-for liberty ;
Then ſhou'd the race of *Iſrael* ſhout for joy,
And their glad tongues in grateful hymns employ.   30

P S A L M *XV.*

1 WHO in thy glorious temple, Lord, ſhall dwell,
     And who ſhall reſt upon thy holy hill ?

2 E'en he, who holds ſimplicity of heart,
And from thy righteous judgments dreads to part ;
Whoſe faithful tongue, indignant of a lie,   5
Wounds not his neighbour's peace with calumny ;
Whoſe thoughts no miſchief 'gainſt a foe intend ;
Who vents no killing ſlander 'gainſt a friend :

4 Who ſhuns the wicked, and deteſts their ways ;
But, honours him, that heav'ns high will obeys ;   10
Who'll to the indigent his help afford,
And loſe his int'reſt, ere he'll break his word.

5 Who with a modeſt income is content,
Nor takes reward againſt the innocent ;
By acts like theſe, who can his duty prove,   15
Shall live for ever with his God above.

P S A L M *XVI.*

1 PRESERVE me, Lord-----on thy bleſt pow'r relies
    My fervent ſoul, and to thy goodneſs flies.

Yet

Yet not to thee my faithful works extend;
Weak tho' I am, an aiding hand I'll lend
To thofe dear faints, in virtue that excel,⁣   5
Their hope, their joy, their pride, with thee to dwell.

4 But haplefs they, who not in thee will truft,
And think their hopes in fancied gods are juft!
Their bloody facrifices I'll difdain,
Nor fhall their impious names my lips profane.   10

5 No; rather in thy pow'r fecure I'll ftand;
Receive my lot, my portion, from thy hand:

6 O bleffed lot! O heavenly retreat! ⁣
In fields of faireft flow'rs is fix'd my feat;
Plac'd as I am therein by hands divine,   15
A fcene of endlefs happinefs is mine.

7 Therefore my foul with gratitude o'erflows;
By thee infpir'd, with heav'nly ardour glows;

8 I feel the prefent God, that guards my fteps;
My high-enraptur'd heart within me leaps;   20
My infirm body trembles with the joy,
And my whole fyftem proves the ecftafy.

10 For from the gloomy horrors of the grave,
Thy *holy*, thy *anointed* one, thou'lt fave;
From dreary darknefs thou his foul wilt free,   25
Nor fhall thy *chofen* vile corruption fee:

11 The blifsful paths of life thou'lt to him fhew,
Where in thy prefence joys for ever flow;
Where in full ftreams immortal pleafures roll,
From thy right-hand, to fill the ravifh'd foul.   30

P S A L M XVII.

1   **D**O thou, juft God, a juft man's pray'r attend;
    O liften to the cry that comes unfeign'd;

2 At thy tribunal *David* afks redrefs,
With pitying eye behold his fad diftrefs.

3 Oft haft thou prov'd me in the filent night,   5
And found the purpofe of my heart was right;
Oft view'd my fecret foul, and found, in nought
My tongue e'er differ'd from my inmoft thought.

4 Thy word my rule, and govern'd by thy fear;
I from the works of impious men kept clear.   10

5 O ftill preferve me in the path I've trod;
O let me firmly tread, all-gracious God.

6 Thee have I oft invok'd, for thou wilt hear;
Lift, while I plead; incline thy gracious ear:

Shew

7 Shew me thy mercy, thou, whofe potent arm   15
   Defends the foul, that trufts in thee, from harm.
8 Thy wings proteƈtful o'er my fteps extend ;
   Me, as the apple of the eye, defend
9 From that abandon'd crew, my peace that wound ;
   From thofe my foes, that compafs me around ;   20
10 Who, with their wealth elate, forget their God,
   And in their guilt are infolently proud.
11 In ev'ry fecret place they lay the fnare ;
   And 'gainft my life their wily fchemes prepare :
12 Like to the lion, that expeƈts his prey,   25
   Or like his whelp, they keep my foul at bay.
13 Arife, O Lord ; confound their villainy ;
   From their deftruƈtive toils thy fervant free ;
14 Thy fword they are ; thy wifdom lets them reign ;
   Thou giv'ft them here a wide, a large domain,   30
   In wealth they flow, and, when they breathe no more,
   Their num'rous fons poffefs their fhining ftore.
15 For me, by innocence of heart I'll ftrive
   Still in thy favour, in thy light, to live ;
   Enough, O gracious God, enough for me   35
   To view in blifs thy glorious majefty.

P S A L M *XVIII.*

1 O SOV'REIGN Lord, whom my fupport I prove,
     Be thou the conftant objeƈt of my love.
2 My rock of fafety thou, my ftrong defence,
   The God, the guardian of my innocence,
   My hope, my folace, in my fore diftrefs,   5
   My fhield, my buckler, when my foes opprefs.
3 Thee I'll invoke ; for worthy thou of praife,
   Thou in her griefs my drooping foul didft raife ;
4 Hemm'd in with dangers, in diftrefs I lay,
   Death with his direful fnares befet my way ;   10
   Down to the dreary fhades, the fields below,
   Caught in his fatal toils, I fear'd to go ;
6 When to my God in confidence I pray'd,
   Preferr'd my fad complaint, implor'd his aid.
7 Nor were my fad complaints in vain preferr'd ;   15
   Soon on his awful throne my voice he heard ;
   Lo ! trembles earth at the vindiƈtive God ;
   Th' affrighted hills from their foundations nod ;
8 From his dread noftrils clouds of fmoke arife ;
   From out his mouth a fire confuming flies ;   20
                                                          He

 9 He bows the Heav'ns; he leaves his awful feat;
　 He comes; thick mifty vapours cloath his feet:
10 " On flaming Cherubs royally he rode;
　 " On wings of winds came flying all abroad ;"
11 Tremendous darknefs his dread prefence fhrouds;
　 Surround him waters, and involve him clouds :　　　25
12 From his bright eyes burft forth a radiant light,
　 That drives the darknefs, and difpels the night;
　 Then falls of rattling hail a dreadful fhow'r,
　 And flakes of fire their glaring volumes pour.　　　30
13 But when the Lord his awful filence broke ;
　 High heav'n with all it's deep artillery fhook;
　 Earth was aftonifh'd at the pouring flood,
　 And with his rapid lightnings æther glow'd.
14 Thro' the vaft void his flaming arrows fly,　　　35
　 And flafh on flafh redoubles, to deftroy :
15 The gaping Earth her fecret fources fhews,
　 Whence fprings the fountain, when the riv'let flows ;
　 And, fo great terror at his wrath fhe feels,
　 Trembling, her own foundations fhe reveals.　　　40
16 He from above reach'd forth his aiding hand ;
　 Me, finking in the waters, he fuftain'd ;
17 Repuls'd the madnefs of my mighty foes,
　 Their wiles eluded, and difpers'd my woes ;
18 And, when with all their malice they affail'd,　　　45
　 Vain were their fchemes-----I in my God prevail'd.
19 Me did he reinftate in liberty,
　 And, 'caufe he lov'd his fervant, fet him free.
20 For well my honeft humble heart he knew,
　 And deem'd the favours he beftow'd, my due :　　　50
21 That in his righteous ways I conftant trod,
　 Nor with the wicked wou'd forfake my God ;
22 His ftatutes long with reverence obey'd,
　 And never from his dread behefts had ftray'd ;
23 Had kept my foul from fraud, from falfhood free,　　　55
　 Had loath'd the paths of guilt, of infamy :
24 Therefore my life with juftice he regards,
　 And with a bounteous hand my truth rewards ;
　 Therefore his favour and his love he fhew'd,
　 And bleffings namelefs, numberlefs, beftow'd.　　　60
25 For who with thee conforms in heart and mind,
　 Thee with the holy fhall they holy find,
　 That to the perfect thou wilt perfect be,
26 And the juft man fhall juftice have from thee :

　　　　　　　　　　　　　　　　　　But

But that the froward fouls, who wilful deal   65
In wily fchemes, fhall thy refentment feel.
27 For, when in mifery the humble grieve,
Thy pow'rful hand is ready to relieve,
And, when with haughty fcorn the wicked glow,
Thou'lt check their high difdain, and bring them low   70
28 Me in adverfity thou'ft oft fuftain'd,
My lamp haft lighted, when the darknefs reign'd.
29 My leader thou, tho' armed hofts affail,
I'll break thro' all, and in thy pow'r prevail:
Sure of Succefs, on their full ranks I'll fall,   75
And fcale the higheft turret of the wall.
30 For, when the righteous, in thy caufe unite,
Thy word is promis'd to defend the right;
Thy word, far purer than the pureft gold,
Clofe, as a buckler, to my breaft I'll hold;   80
With firmeft hope I'll on thy word rely,
Spring on the foe, and fnatch the victory:
31 For who is Lord, or who is God, but thee?
Who elfe has pow'r, has might, has majefty?
32 Thou giv'ft me ftrength againft the foe, O God;   85
To heav'nly wifdom pointeft out the road;
33 Thou giv'ft me, fwifter than the hart to fly,
And far from danger placeft me on high:
34 Inftruct'ft my hand, the ufe of arms to know,
To dart the jav'lin, and to wield the bow.   90
35 My rock of fafety thou, my pow'rful might;
Thy ftrong right-hand protects me in the fight;
36 Thou clear'ft my road thro' the impervious way;
My tott'ring Feet, where fnares entrap, doft ftay;
37 Doft to my foul true fortitude impart;   95
Soon feel my fainting foes the deadly dart;
38 Soon at my feet my mercy they implore,
Sink with their wounds, and fall, to rife no more.
39 Thro' all my limbs new ftrength doft thou infufe;
My ardent foul the gen'rous chace purfues;   100
40 I'm all on fire; my foes I foon deftroy;
Difmay'd, dejected, from my arms they fly;
41 They call for fuccour, but no fuccour's near;
To thee they call, but thou difdain'ft to hear;
42 Swift, I purfue, and follow clofe behind;   105
Swift they difperfe, like duft before the wind;
And, like the filthy rubbifh of the ftreet,
I fpurn their bodies with triumphant feet.

Thus

43 Thus from their hoſtile rage thou ſet'ſt me free,
  And crown'ſt me with imperial dignity ;   110
  E'en o'er the *heathen* giv'ſt unbounded ſway,
  ¹ And bidſt the diſtant realms my rule obey ;
44 The diſtant realms ſubmiſſive own my right,
45 Diſtruſt their caſtles, and decline the fight.
46 Praiſe, might and majeſty to thee, O Lord ;   115
  Thou didſt thy pow'rful help to me afford ;
47 Didſt 'gainſt my foes my injur'd cauſe maintain,
  And gav'ſt me o'er thy favour'd tribes to reign ;
48 Thou bidſt the tumults of the wicked ceaſe,
  Diſtract'ſt their counſels, and commandeſt peace ;   120
49 Therefore amid the nations I'll proclaim,
  In ſongs of gratitude, thy glorious name ;
50 For to thy *choſen*, thy anointed king
  Didſt thou, in his diſmay, deliv'rance bring,
  Haſt crown'd his days with glory and ſucceſs,   125
  And ſtill his lateſt progeny wilt bleſs.

P S A L M *XIX.*

1 THE ſpacious firmament, that hangs on high,
    The ſplendid glories of the ſpangled ſky,
Fix'd in due order, clad in bright array,
  The great, th' almighty architect, diſplay.
2 From day to day, from night to night, they roll,   5
  And pour conviction on the humble ſoul :
3 In them, ſurpriz'd, the various nations hear
  The mighty God his ruling pow'r declare :
4 To regions moſt remote aloud they found ;
  Their voice extends to earth's extremeſt bound.   10
5 High 'bove the reſt, in his full radiance gay,
  Comes forth th' englad'ning ſun, to gild the day ;
  Like a young bridegroom, who, to charm his fair,
  Adorns his body with the niceſt care ;
  Exulting, like a giant, in his force,   15
  He runs with vaſt rapidity, his courſe.
6 See, from the eaſt his roſy car he drives ;
  Lo ! nature at his joyous beams revives ;
  See, o'er the wide *expanſe* he wheels his way ;
  The whole creation at his preſence gay.   20
7 But not alone theſe wonders ſtrike with awe ;
  The Lord's as glorious in his ſacred law ;
  His laws, which ſtricteſt purity impart,
  His word that giveth wiſdom to the heart ;

His

8 His ſtatutes that rejoice the humble ſoul,   25
  His judgments that the ways of ſin controul,
  His precepts that enlight the pious breaſt,
  His holy fear, that ſhall for ever laſt.
10 With them not e'en the richeſt ſweets compare ;
  Than gold, than gems, of nobler price they are ;   30
11 By them thy ſervant rules his inmoſt thought,
  And the bright road to happineſs is taught.
12 Yet who the errors of his heart can tell,
  How oft 'gainſt thee his ſecret thoughts rebel ;
  What vain *ideas* in his fancy play,   35
  And o'er each word, each action, hold the ſway ?
  O cleanſe thy ſervant from the great offence ;
13 O let him keep his truth, his innocence ;
  O from preſumptuous guilt preſerve him free,
  And firm him in his own ſimplicity.   40
14 Grant, dear redeemer, this my fervent pray'r ;
  Whate'er my words, my meditations are,
  To thee may they, a grateful incenſe, riſe,
  And meet with kind acceptance from thy eyes.

P S A L M *XX.*

1 WHEN troubles hem thee round, when foes diſtreſs,
    And thou to heav'n thy fervent pray'r addreſs,
  To thee a liſt'ning ear th' almighty lend,
  Thee by his name may *Jacob*'s God defend :
2 From his reſplendent throne aſſiſtance give,   5
  From *Sion*'s ſacred temple bid thee live ;
3 Thy victims at his altar not forget ;
  And thy oblations graciouſly accept ;
4 Grant to thy heart's deſire the aſk'd ſucceſs,
  Diſpel thy woes, and all thy counſels bleſs.   10
5 And when th' almighty God has given his aid,
  And crown'd with conqueſt thy anointed head,
  We'll join thy triumphs with according voice,
  And in thy great deliv'rer we'll rejoice.
6 For well we know thou art th' eternal's care,   15
  That from his lofty throne thy ſuit he'll hear ;
  That not in vain thou'lt on his pow'r rely ;
  His ſtrong right-hand will give thee victory.
7 Let the proud *heathen* in their cars confide,
  And on their harneſt'd ſteeds exulting ride ;   20
  Be they their empty boaſt-----more wiſely we
  Depend, O God, on thy great name and thee.

1 SAV'D by thy hand, triumphant in thy pow'r,
The king shall thee in gratitude adore.
By thee supported in the doubtful day,
To thee the tribute of his praise shall pay:
2 Ne'er, when with suppliant voice to thee he pray'd,   5
Didst thou deny in his distress thy aid;
Ne'er, when his lips pour'd forth his heart's desire,
Fruitless did he the humble boon require.
3 Of all the bounties of thy love possest,
Above the warmest of his wishes blest,   10
A golden diadem surrounds his head,
Whose glitt'ring gems their bright effulgence shed.
4 For life he ask'd-----thou more than life hast giv'n,
A life of immortality in heav'n.
5 Eternal honours does thy hand bestow;   15
Eternal glories from thy goodness flow;
6 Eternal bliss thou giv'st without alloy,
Thy glad'ning presence ever to enjoy.
7 For thou the anchor of his hope shalt be;
His trust he'll place, all-pow'rful God, in thee.   20
8 Thy foes thy hand vindictive soon shall feel;
Vainly from thee wou'd they themselves conceal;
9 For, like the fire, which in the furnace roars,
And the dry fuel, greedily devours,
On their devoted heads thy judgments fall,   25
And thy tremendous wrath consumes them all;
10 Their names are lost among the sons of men,
And none will dare to say they've ever been.
11 'Gainst thee their fraudful villainies they schem'd;
And, boastful, of their high success they dream'd: 30
12 Therefore from thee shall they attempt to fly,

So fhall the pious tribes thy name adore,   35
And in continued anthems hail thy pow'r.

P S A L M *XXII.*

1 WHY does my God forfake me? will no more
      Thy goodnefs aid me, when I life implore?
2 The tedious day, the live-long night I figh;
   In vain; thy faving pow'r does ftill deny.
3 Yet art thou holy, O thou fov'reign king;   5
   Thy praife the fons of *Sion* conftant fing;
4 On thee our fathers in their woes relied,
   On thee they call'd, nor was thy aid denied.
5 Their only folace in their fore diftrefs,
   Benign thou heard'ft their pray'r, and didft redrefs.   10
6 But I'm a worm-----no man am I-----the croud
   With jeers infult me, and reproach aloud;
7 With killing fcorn, who meet me in the way,
   Shoot out the lip and fhake the head, and fay;
8 " In God he plac'd his empty confidence;   15
   " The Lord he boafted for his fure defence;
   " Since Heav'n his glory, his delight he made,
   " Let him fupport him now, and grant him aid."
9 But fure, when in the dreary womb I lay,
   Thy goodnefs gave me, to enjoy the day;   20
   When a weak helplefs infant at the breaft,
   Thou waft my God, and with thy favour bleft:
11 Now then, when only thou canft comfort give,
   Let me fecure in thy protection live.
12 Wild bulls of *Bafhan* compafs me around;   25
   Me they befet, and meditate the wound;
13 On me they gape, and threaten to devour,
   And, like to fierce and famifh'd lions, roar.
14 My blood flows out; fhrunk up is ev'ry vein;
   My feeble joints, my body fcarce fuftain;   30
   My trembling tortur'd heart forgets to beat;
   It melts, like wax diffolving in the heat:
15 Like a mere potfherd, am I dried away;
   My ftrength is loft; my weaken'd limbs decay;
   Clofe to my fhrivel'd jaws my tongue does cleave,   35
   And lo! I totter o'er the gaping grave.
16 For the whole impious rout enclofe me round;
   And, like fell wolves, my wretched body wound.
17 They pierce my hands-----my feet-----fo lank I'm grown,
   With eafe may be diftinguifh'd bone from bone.   40

With

With the fad view they glut their rav'ning eye,
And feed their cruel hearts with horrid joy.
18. My various garments 'mongft them they divide,
  And, whofe my vefture, by the lot is tried.
19 But, gracious Lord, thy pleading fervant hear,   45
  And hafte my fad afflicted foul to chear,
20 Drive back the fword of my affaulting foes ;
  The fury of thefe rav'ning wolves oppofe ;
21 O fave me, fave me from the lions jaws,
  And with thy ftrongeft might fupport my caufe.   50
22 From death redeem'd, thy goodnefs I'll proclaim,
  And in the glad affembly hymn thy name.
23 Ye humble fouls, that fear the Lord, rejoice ;
  Ye fons of *Jacob*, raife the tuneful voice ;
  In feftal hymns fet forth his faving pow'r,   55
  In fongs of joy his clemency adore :
24 For, when th' afflicted in fad anguifh cried,
  With fcorn he heard not, nor his aid denied ;
  Nor from his mis'ries turn'd his face away,
  But to his troubled foul reftor'd the day.   60
25 Therefore his praifes fhall employ my tongue,
  And all the pious tribes fhall join the fong.
26 The humbly meek, that feek th' almighty Lord,
  Who've long his glorious attributes ador'd,
  With joy fhall at his facred banquet feed,   65
  And fatisfy their foul with living bread.
27 Yes ; all the nations of the world fhall own
  His pow'r, fhall worfhip 'fore his awful throne ;
  Earth's fartheft bounds his ftatutes fhall obey,
  And with according voice avow his fway :   70
28 Earth's fartheft bounds are fubject to his pow'r,

P S A L M *XXIII.*

1 " **T**H E bounteous Lord my paſtures ſhall prepare,
  "   And feed his ſervant with a ſhepherd's care :"
2 In a gay verdant plain, with flow'rs o'erſpread,
  Where *nature* furniſhes her ſofteſt bed ;
  Where the clear ſtream in ſmooth meanders flows,   5
  He bids me take a ſweet, ſerene repoſe.
3 When in erroneous paths I ſimply ſtray,
  His gracious goodneſs leads me in the way ;
  Recals my wand'ring ſteps, and points the road,
  The even path his *David* ſhou'd have trod.   10
4 Yea ; tho' the gloomy vale of death I tread,
  Where dreary horrors compaſs round my head,
  E'en there no fatal ills my ſoul betide,
  Thy rod, thy ſtaff, my comfort and my guide.
5 Vainly my foes with hell-born envy burn ;   15
  The choiceſt cates my loaded board adorn,
  My chearful bowls are fill'd with pureſt wine,
  And round my brows thy richeſt ointments ſhine.
6 And, while my breath inſpires this vital clay,
  On thee ſecure I'll reſt, for ever gay ;   20
  Thy truth, thy mercy, ſhall protect me ſtill,
  And conſtant I'll attend thy holy hill.

P S A L M . *XXIV.*

1 **T**H E ſpacious earth, and what the earth contains,
    Are heav'n's high Lord's----o'er the wide world he
  O'er the wide world extends his boundleſs ſway ;   [reigns;
  The wild, the wiſe, the wretched and the gay,
  The poor, the rich, howe'er diſpers'd they are,   5
  Are *his*, and feel his providential care.
2 He on the ſeas this ſolid earth hath plac'd ;
  He on the raging floods has fix'd her faſt ;
  In vain the waters riſe, the billows roar,
  He braves their fury, and defies their pow'r.   10
3 All then is God's-----but one empyreal throne,
  Sublime above all heights, has made his own.
  Thither can man aſcend ? is man ſo bleſt,
  As near his maker on his hill to reſt ?
4 Yes ; he whoſe honeſt heart from guilt is clear,   15
  Whoſe hands are ſpotleſs, and his tongue ſincere ;
  Who ſhuns of *vanity* the baneful road,
  Nor to deceitful oaths atteſts his God ;

                                   He

7 Ye doors, that on eternal hinges turn,
Ye fhining gatés, which fparkling gems adorn;
The king of glory comes, by all ador'd,   25
Ope wide your portals and receive your Lord.
8 This king of glory who? what royal gueft
In thefe our facred manfions deigns to reft?
E'en he, the mighty God, whofe ftrong right-hand
Has o'er th' extended univerfe command;   30
Whofe force in vain embattl'd ranks oppofe,
Who comes triumphant o'er his vanquifh'd foes.
9 Ye doors that on eternal hinges turn,
Ye fhining gates, which fparkling gems adorn;
The king of glory comes, by all ador'd;   35
Ope wide your portals, and receive your Lord.
10 This king of glory who?-----enquire no more-----
That fov'reign *being* of unbounded pow'r;
That God encircled round with majefty-----
The Lord of hofts-----the king of glory, he.   40

P S A L M XXV.

1 TO thee alone, O fov'reigh Lord, I cry;
2 On thee alone, my gracious God, rely;
O free my foul from fhame, nor let my foes
Infulting fay; a vain fupport I chofe.
3 No; meet not they, that wait on thee, with fhame;   5
That love thy ftatutes, that revere thy name:
Be fhame their deftin'd lot, who thee defpife;
Who truft in fraud, in villainy, in lies.
4 Me in life's devious road benignly lead,
That I fecurely in thy paths may tread;   10
5 Shew me thy truth, and teach me, not to ftray;
Thy ftrength my truft, thy pow'rful word my ftay.
6 Remember, Lord, (nor be thy fervant bold)
Thy mercies and thy clemencies of old;
7 But ah! remember not my youthful crimes,   15
The faults and follies of my wilder times,
When paffion's lure had led my heart away;
And from thy facred laws I dar'd to ftray;
Thefe, Lord, remember not; let mercy plead,
And bid thy goodnefs to thy wrath fucceed.   20

Benign

8 Benign art thou, and when, all-clement God,
  Vile man repents, thou point'ft the heavenly road.
9 The meek, the modeft, thy affiftance prove,
  Follow the right, nor in blind error rove:
10 Their kind director thou, who love thy law,   25
  And keep thy ftatutes with religious awe,
  From fin, from forrow, fhall they walk exempt,
  No griefs fhall touch them, and no paffions tempt.
11 That I may then to after-times proclaim,
  To regions moft remote, thy facred name,   30
  Great tho' they be, my num'rous fins forgive,
  And in thy mercy let thy *David* live.
12 O happy they, who're govern'd by thy fear !
  To help them on to truth, thou'rt always near;
13 Their fouls with affluence and with peace to blefs;   35
  Their fons to crown with glory and fuccefs;
14 To them thy facred myfteries to reveal,
  The fecret counfels of thy will to tell.
15 Therefore my tearful eyes I raife to thee;
  Reft all my hopes upon thy clemency;   40
  'Tis thou alone canft clear me from the net
  My cruel foes have laid, t' enfnare my feet.
16 O turn thee to me, and thy mercy fhew;
  For deep I'm funk in wretchednefs, in woe;
17 Inceffant griefs my harraft foul diftrefs;   45
  O hear me, and reftore my wonted peace:
18 With eyes of pity my fad anguifh view;
  Nor let thy vengeance ftill my crimes purfue.
19 Great are my foes, their malice greater ftill,
  And from their ceafelefs hate what pangs I feel ?   50
20 No more their fport, their laughter, let me be,
  But fpare me, fave me, for I truft in thee.
21 On thy integrity I'll yet rely,
  And fure thy goodnefs will not let me die:
22 No; gracious God, thy mercy thou'lt difplay,   55
  And free the pious tribes, who thee obey.

P S A L M   XXVI.

1 TO thee, O fov'reign father, I appeal;
    To thee the fecrets of my foul reveal,
  My faithful foul, that, firm in innocence,
  Makes thee her fureft hope, her ftrong defence.
2 O try thy fervant, fcrutinize his heart;   5
  Prove him, and judge according to defert.

With

3 'With grateful eyes thy mercies all I view,
 With careful fteps the road to truth purfue ;
4 The fraudful tongue, that ruins with a lie,
 The idly vain, that love not thee, I fly ; 10
5 The converfe of ungodly men I hate,
 Nor 'mid the wicked e'er will fix my feat.
6 With hands unftain'd I'll at thy altar bow,
 There pay the adoration that I owe ;
7 In thankful hymns I'll there employ my voice, 15
 And in the wonders of my God rejoice :
8 I love the temple, where thy name's ador'd ;
 Much do I love thy hallow'd dome, O Lord.
9 Then fuffer not my foul, to fhades below,
 With bloody, with deceitful men, to go ; 20
10 With men, whofe hands in mifchiefs are involv'd,
 Whofe hearts for gain the blackeft crimes refolv'd.
11 No; my fincerity be ftill my guard,
 With thy redemption my firm foul reward ;
12 Firm that fhe ftands, Lowe, my God, to thee : 25
 Thy name be prais'd thro' all eternity.

P S A L M XXVII.

1 MY light, my great falvation is the Lord ;
  While he his ftrong affiftance will afford ;
While he, to aid, to comfort me, is near,
No open force, no hidden fraud, I fear.
2 Me, with big hopes, my wicked foes affail'd ; 5
 In vain ; their haughty expectations fail'd :
 'Gainft me their various treach'ries they prepar'd ;
 And fell themfelves, in their own toils enfnar'd.
3 Tho' wars fhou'd threaten, and tho' camps furround,
 Tho' hoftile bands fhou'd meditate the wound ; 10
 Amid the danger, free from fear, my heart
 Wou'd brave the battle, and defy the dart.
4 One boon alone I've afk'd, and ftill defire,
 That, while my breath this vital clay infpire,
 I in the temple of my God may dwell, 15
 The wonders of his mighty hand may tell ;
 The beauty of his holinefs furvey,
 And humble, ardent adoration pay.
5 For in diftrefs his fervant he'll fecure,
 My foul in fafety from the foe enfure, 20
 Will his pavilion make my ftrong retreat ;
 And on a rock will firmly fix my feet :

6 And now, above my foes exalted, I
My hours in grateful praifes will employ,
My victims to his facred altar bring,   25
And *allelujahs* to my faviour fing.

7 Hear me, my God; to thee I fuppliant cry;
All-clement Lord, thy mercy not deny;

8 'Tis thy command, that we fhou'd feek thy face;
With eager foul I that command embrace;   30

9 Thy face not hide in anger from my eyes;
In danger, in diftrefs, on thee relies
Thy troubled fervant; chafe his griefs away,
Difpel his darknefs, and reftore the day.

10 When father, mother, friends forfake, then thou   35
Will to my foul thy tender mercies fhew.

11 Do thou benignly lead me in the way,
Left, by my foes deluded, I fhou'd ftray;

12 By them around befet, I've none but thee,
My heart from error, from diftrefs, to free.   40
'Gainft me with forged calumnies they rife,
And perfecute my foul with cruel lies.

13 And furely I fhou'd to my miferies yield,
If not by hope, by faith in thee, upheld.
No longer dubious, in that hope I live,   45
Affur'd, at length thou'lt kind affiftance give.

14 Therefore, my foul, in confidence of pray'r,
Bravely bear up, and caft on God thy care;
Thee will he ftrengthen to fupport thy grief:
----Wait on the Lord, and thou wilt have relief.   50

P S A L M   *XXVIII.*

1 O THOU fupreme, that ruleft over all;
My rock of fafety, hear me, when I call;
Left I be number'd with the filent dead,
" Who wake no more, the vital fpirit fled."

2 Hear, when with earneft voice to thee I plain;   5
Be not my faithful pray'r addreft in vain;
With hands uplifted I my fuit prefer;
Out of thy high *etherial* temple hear;

3 join not thy fervant with that wicked croud,
In fin who wallow, and who hate the good;   10
Whofe foothing tongues foft founds of concord yield,
But whofe vile hearts with villain-thoughts are fill'd.

4 Reward them, Lord, juft as their deeds require;
Give them, t' enjoy of wickednefs the hire;

Give

Therefore with ardent gratitude fhe glows,
And my enraptur'd tongue with praifes flows.
8 For, as the fwain his fleecy flock does tend,
 Doft thou the people, thou haft chofe, defend;
 And thy anointed king in his diftrefs
 Benign affift, and with deliv'rance blefs.
9 O ftill preferve them; be they ftill thy care;
 And let their progeny thy goodnefs fhare;
 Feed them in peace; protect them with thy pow'r,
 Be thou their God, till time fhall be no more.

PSALM XXIX.

1 YE mighty potentates, enthron'd on high,
    Ye warrior-chieftains, crown'd with victory;
 Not to yourfelves attribute the fuccefs;
 Give God the glory, and his goodnefs blefs.
2 His ftrong right-hand in grateful fongs proclaim,   5
 Shout forth his praifes, and extol his name.
3 His voice majeftic, never heard in vain,
 Sends down, to glad the earth, the fleecy rain;
 His voice is in the rumbling thunder heard;
 And in the red impetuous lightning fear'd;   10
 Revere his voice, the ftormy winds, that fweep,
 The mad'ning waves that bellow in, the deep.
 Lo! lofty *Lebanon* exults no more;
 Their fcatter'd boughs her cedars now deplore;
 Th' almighty fpeaks, their tow'ring honours fall,   15
 To his tremendous voice fubmiffive all:
 At his command e'en firmeft mountains move,

All earth, all heav'n, his wondrous glory own,
And fall with rev'rence 'fore his awful throne :

10 Revere him all the waters of the main,   25
And the whole univerſe avows his reign.

11 Nor cauſeleſs they avow-----to all that pay
Due rev'rence to his will, his laws obey,
Will he, th' aſſiſtance of his mercy give,
And in eternal affluence bid them live.   30

P S. A L M *XXX.*

1 IN hymns of praiſe will I employ my tongue ;
My tuneful harp ſhall anſwer to the ſong.
To thee, O Lord ; for, when with pain diſtreſt,
And foes around their cruel joy expreſt,
Me in the evil day didſt thou ſuſtain,   5
My foes indulg'd their impious hopes in vain.

2 Struck with the dire diſeaſe, to thee I cried ;
Nor was, O God, thy healing hand denied ;

3 For from the dreary horrors of the grave,
When he implor'd, didſt thou thy ſervant ſave,   10
His ſoul, juſt hov'ring o'er the pit retrieve,
And gav'ſt again, in joyous health to live.

4 O all ye ſaints, his gracious goodneſs ſing ;
Diſplay his praiſes on the trembling ſtring ;

5 For but a moment his dread anger lives,   15
While life, his quick-returning favour gives ;
And, tho' the night in ſighs, in tears, you ſpend,
The dawning morn will all your ſorrows end.

6 Surpriz'd with my ſucceſs, elate with pride,
Big with my empty ſelf, I fondly cried ;   20
" Strong in my happineſs, my foes I dare,
" Nor open force, nor ſecret fraud, I fear."

7 By heav'n ſupported, like a mountain firm,
That braves the thunder, and diſdains the ſtorm,
Did I the angry bolts of fate deride,   25
And wrapt my heart in arrogance and pride ;
But ſoon the folly of my ways I found,
Loſt thy ſupport, and felt a killing wound.

8 'Twas then my reaſon to my ſoul return'd ;
In deep repentance I my madneſs mourn'd ;   30
For thy forgiveneſs humbly ſued, O Lord,
My guilt acknowledg'd, and thy aid implor'd.

9 " What profit is there (ſaid I) in my blood ?
" Juſtly thy vengeance has my crimes purſued.

" But

    " But can the *dead* thy wondrous works proclaim ?   35.
    " Can duſt, can *aſhes*, celebrate thy name ?
10 " O hear me, hear me, and thy mercy ſhew ;
    " Redeem my ſoul from death, my life from woe."
11 Nor vainly did I pray ; thy mercy heard ;
    My fainting ſoul in all her ſorrows chear'd,
    My grief to joy, my tears to laughter turn'd ;   40
    No more I languiſh'd, and no more I mourn'd.
12 Therefore thy goodneſs will I conſtant ſing,
    And to thy glorious name attune the ſtring ;
    Therefore in hymns harmonious I'll diſplay   45
    Thy clemency ; thy love, from day to day.

P S A L M *XXXI.*

1 IN thee, O God, my conſtant truſt I place ;
    Let not thy faithful ſervant meet diſgrace ;
2 Exert thy juſtice, and benignly hear ;
    Guide me in ſafety, and diſpel my fear ;
    Thou art my tow'r of ſtrength ; my rock art thou ;   5
    Be ſtill my rock ; my tow'r of ſtrength be now.
4 On thee relying, ſhall I be diſmay'd ?
    O ſave me from the ſecret net they've laid.
5 My great redeemer thou, ſecure I'll ſtand
    Beneath the ſhelter of thy mighty hand :   10
6 My truſt the dread *Jehovah* ; I deſpiſe
    The fools that deal in vanity and lies ;
7 Yes ; in thy mercy ſhall my ſoul rejoice ;
    Oft in her troubles haſt thou heard her voice ;
8 Oft, when her foes aſſail'd, haſt ſet her free,   15
    And giv'n my fetter'd feet full liberty.
9 But now in bitterneſs of heart I mourn ;
    And humbly to the God of mercy turn ;
    Mine eyes with conſtant, ſcalding tears decay ;
    Pines my ſad ſoul ; my body wears away ;   20
10 My life is ſpent with griefs, my years in ſighs ;
    Wither my bones ; my ſtrength within me dies.
11 My foes inſult me, and deride my woe ;
    My neighbours round a mean abhorrence ſhew ;
    Nay ; e'en my friends for fear come not anigh,   25
    And, when they ſee me at a diſtance, fly.
12 As one among the dead, I'm quite forgot,
    Sink beneath notice ; and am really nought :
13 Their ſlanders, their foul calumnies I hear ;
    On ev'ry ſide ſurrounds me ev'ry fear ;   30

Their bafe devices 'gainſt my life I know,
And what their ſecret malice dooms me to.

14 Yet ſtill, O Lord, on thee I've fix'd my truſt;
My God I'll call thee, for thou ſtill art juſt:

15 Thou rul'ſt my life; it's term depends on thee;   35
O free me from the cruel enemy:

16 Bright on thy ſervant, let thy goodneſs ſhine,
And ſhield me with thy clemency divine:

17 Thy help implor'd, let me not ſink in ſhame;
Be that their deſtin'd lot, that hate thy name: 40.
That love a lie, are cruel, vain and proud,
And vent their horrid ſlanders 'gainſt the good:
Let them, juſt God, of ſhame their portion have;
And ſleep in dreadful ſilence in the grave.

19 How great thy goodneſs? how thy bounties flow   45
On all that to thy laws obedience ſhew?
'Fore all the earth, what wonders haſt thou wrought
For them that rev'rence thee in act, in thought?

20 In vain the pow'rful wicked vaunt their pride;
Them from their malice thou'lt ſecurely hide;   50
In vain the pois'nous tongue aſſaults their fame;
A ſafe protection in thy houſe they claim.

21 Eternal praiſe, eternal thanks, O Lord;
For wondrous was the aid thou didſt afford;
Not armed hoſts, not ſtrongeſt tow'rs can prove   55
Such ſure defence, as yields thy pow'rful love.

22 Void of ſupport, quite comfortleſs and poor,
I ſaid, deſpairing; " All my hopes are o'er;"
When thou the voice of my complaint didſt hear,
And in my worſt diſtreſs diſpell'dſt my fear.   60

24 Therefore, ye pious ſouls, ye truly juſt,
Love well the Lord, and in his goodneſs truſt;
For he'll the *proud* ones of the earth deſtroy,
And bleſs the humble with immortal joy.

25 Be brave, be dauntleſs then; purſue the road,   65
The path that leads you to the throne of God;
With ſteady feet go on; on him depend;
Crown'd are our labours, when our God's our friend.

P S A L M *XXXII.*

1 THRICE happy he, whoſe ſins his God forgives;
His crimes in deep oblivion loſt, who lives;

2 Whoſe ſlips, whoſe failings are not counted *his*;
Whoſe ſoul perverſely does not act amiſs!

For

3 For me, while I my fecret faults conceal'd,
  While not the errors of my life reveal'd,
  A tabid weaknefs feiz'd my languid bones,
  The tedious hours I fpent in piteous moans ;
4 Thy heavy hand I felt by night, by day, 10
  And all my juices melted quick away.
5 Soon then to thee, O gracious God, I turn'd,
  My many crimes, my various errors mourn'd ;
  Soon then to thee I all my fins confeft,
  And ftrait with pardon from thy love was bleft.
6 For this the pious heart, the foul fincere, 15
  In fitting time fhall fly to thee in pray'r;
  Nor, tho' the rifing floods this earth o'erfpread,
  Shall they the threat'nings of the billows dread.
7 My fure defence, my certain refuge thou,
  No griefs, no perils, can o'er-whelm me now; 20
  My foul doft thou replenifh with thy joy,
  And all my woes, and all my terrors fly.
8 Nay more; thou kindly promifeft thy aid ;
  " Mine hand (thou crieft) fhall point thee where to tread;
  " Mine eye fhall guide thee in the perfect way; 25
  " And round thy feet I'll beam continued day.
9 " But thou the reftiff mule refemble not,
  " The fierce impetuous fteed, devoid of thought,
  " Which, if not govern'd by the bitted rein,
  " Wou'd rove in favage liberty the plain." 30
10 His gracious goodnefs this; fuch mercy they
   Have from their God, who his high will obey.
   While dread tremendous punifhments await
   The wretch that in his crimes is obftinate.
11 Come then, ye righteous fouls, indulge your joy, 35
   In tuneful hymns your happy hours employ;
   Be God the object of your love, your truft ;
   And in his faving pow'r rejoice, ye juft.

P S A L M *XXXIII.*

1 O ALL ye good, who heav'n-born juftice love,
    The Lord *Jehovah* fing, that rules above ;
  Your great creator joyfully extol ;
  The bleft employ befits the pious foul.
2 Strike, ftrike the lute, in honour of his name ; 5
  His praife the ten-ftring'd pfaltery proclaim ;
3 In fweet harmonious fong the voice employ,
  And let the clarion join the general joy.

For

4 For his all-pow'rful word the right commands,
  And righteous are the wonders of his hands;   10

5. His love to juſtice and to truth he ſhews,
  And o'er the ſpacious globe his goodneſs flows.

6 He ſpoke, and ſtraitway into being ſprung,
  High heav'n, with all it's radiant glories hung;

7 He ſpoke; the waters of the main obey'd,   15
  Shrunk within bounds, and in the depths were laid.

8 Thou too, O earth, thy great creator fear,
  And bid thy ſcatter'd ſons his name revere;

9 For at his word firm thy foundation ſtood;
  From his beheſt thy ev'ry bleſſing flow'd.   20

10 'Tis he confounds of impious men the ſchemes;
  He bids; they fleet away like morning-dreams:

11 While firm and fix'd his counſels ſtill remain,
  And all th' aſſaults of time 'gainſt them are vain.

12 That nation's doubly bleſt, whoſe God's the Lord;   25
  What nobler grace can heav'n's high king afford,
  Than ſuch peculiar favour to us ſhown,
  To chuſe us thus, and ſeal us for his own?

13 From his celeſtial throne th' all-ſeeing God
  Looks down, and caſts his awful eye abroad;   30
  The ſons of men in all their ſecrets views;
  Their ſchemes thro' all their *labyrinths* purſues;

15 He forms the cloſe receſſes of the mind,
  And he each lurking thought therein can find.

16 Earth's haughty potentates confide in vain   35
  In armed turrets and in hoſts of men;
  The valiant chieftain, in his proweſs proud,
  In vain his ſtrength, his courage boaſts aloud:

17 And oft, tho' fleeter than the wind his ſpeed,
  Deceives in battle, the impetuous ſteed.   40

18 While God, all-pow'rful, with a watchful eye,
  Looks down on thoſe, who on his aid rely;

19 Their ſouls, when famine threatens, to relieve;
  From death's dark dreary horrors to reprieve.

20 Therefore on his beneficence we'll wait,   45
  Our ſhield, our ſure defence, in ev'ry ſtrait:

21 To him, 'cauſe never he'll our hopes deceive,
  Our hearts the tribute of their praiſe ſhall give.

22 Thy mercy, Lord, ſhall on thy ſervants ſhine;
  On thee our hopes are fix'd, and we are thine.   50

PSALM

P S A L M *XXXIV.*

1 WHILST life, great God, thou giv'ft me to enjoy,
    Thy praifes fhall my grateful tongue employ;
2 Thy pow'r my boaft; thy pow'r I'll long difplay;
With me, ye meek, indulge the pleafing lay,
With me to him your voice alternate raife;   5
Gladly you'll join my fervent heart in praife.
4 Oft when I've pray'd, he lent a gracious ear,
And freed my troubled foul from ev'ry fear;
5 Whoe'er invok'd his name, but he reliev'd?
Who met repulfe, when to their God they griev'd?   10
6 Did e'er the poor a fruitlefs aid implore?
No; when they call'd on him, they griev'd no more.
7 Who fear his word, who reverence his laws,
He fends his angel to fupport their caufe.
8 O tafte and fee-----you'll find, our God is juft;   15
Thrice happy they, that in his mercy truft!
9 Ye pious fouls, put up a faithful pray'r,
And you his kind beneficence fhall fhare:
10 While, roar the lion's favage young for food,
Our God is to the righteous ever good.   20
11 Come then, ye thoughtlefs, liften to my lore,
And you to virtue's high rewards fhall foar;
12 Say, wou'dft thou live a happy length of days,
Void of all ill, in opulence and eafe?
13 Thy tongue from lies, from perjuries, reftrain,   25
And ev'ry vile infidious fraud difdain;
14 From ev'ry fin of ev'ry fort depart;
With ev'ry virtue fanctify thy heart.
15 For on the righteous cafts our God his eye;
His pitying ears he opens to their cry;   30
16 But from obdurate finners turns his face,
Their name and their memorial to erafe.
17 When prays the juft, the good, he always hears;
Is always ready to difpel their fears;
18 Their hearts, juft broken with their griefs, to aid,   35
Their fouls to free, when cruel foes invade.
19 Many the mis'ries that affault their peace,
Yet ftill their guardian God will give them eafe;
20 Amid the various perils that furround,
Vig'rous and brave and refolute they're found: 40
21 By their own crimes while wicked men fhall fall,
And, foes to innocence, fhall perifh all;

22 Our God will them, that worſhip him, defend,
And ne'er defert them, till their lives ſhall end.

P S A L M *XXXV.*

1 MY injur'd cauſe, my great protector, plead;
And 'gainſt invet'rate foes thy ſervant aid:
2 Arm, arm, put on the buckler and the ſhield;
3 Arm, arm, and meet them in th' embattl'd field;
O bid my ſoul to rid her of her fear;   5
Tell her, her great deliverer is near.
4 With bitter ſhame, with foul difgrace meet they,
Who with infidious ſnares befet my way;
In ſure confuſion all their ſchemes involve,
Whoſe vile invenom'd hearts my death refolve.   10
5 Let thy avenging angel preſs them cloſe,
While they (like chaff, that, when the tempeſt blows,
Is driv'n far and wide) with terror fly;
Yet be no aid, no kind protector, nigh:
Their path be ſlipp'ry, and let night ſurround;   15
To death let thy avenging angel wound.
7 For, cauſeleſs, they their ſecret ſnares have laid;
Me to deſtroy, they lurk in ambuſcade.
8 But let their hidden toils themſelves enſnare,
Be theirs the ruin, they for me prepare.   20
9 Then ſhall my ſoul ſincerely taſte her joy;
Shall feel her happineſs without alloy:
10 My bones ſhall cry; " my God, who's like to thee,
" That doſt the humble from oppreſſion free,
" That curb'ſt of lawleſs tyranny the pow'r,   25
" And bidſt the broken heart to grieve no more?"
11 'Gainſt me their cruel enmity not dies;
'Gainſt me with curſed virulence they riſe,
Lay to my charge unheard-of villainy,
And load my guiltleſs ſoul with infamy: 30
12 With bitter hatred all my friendſhip pay,
And my perdition work by night, by day.
13 Not ſo did I-----when ſickneſs ſore oppreſt,
And hov'ring death their anguiſh'd hearts diſtreſt,
In ſackcloth I, in aſhes for them moan'd;   35
For them I faſted, and for them I groan'd;
Quick flow'd my tears; to thee I proſtrate pray'd,
That thou'dſt not number them among the dead.
14 So, when a dear-lov'd friend or brother dies,
The ſoul ſincere with killing anguiſh ſighs;   40

With forrow thus is pain'd the pious fon,
The tender object of his duty gone.

15 Soon they repay'd me with ingratitude;
When fwift calamity my fteps purfued,
They all rejoic'd, and, at my mis'ries gay, 45
They danc'd, they revell'd, they kept holiday;
Their villain-feafts the very *abjects* join'd,
And there with them my ruin they defign'd;

16 Yes; mere buffoons their vile affociates were,
Who grinn'd their malice with an envious fneer. 50

17 But, Lord, how long wilt thou thy patience fhew,
And view with feeming unconcern my woe?
From their deftructive wiles relieve my foul:
Their cruel fchemes, their vile attempts controul:

18 Then in the great affembly I will fing 55
Thy praife, and to thy glory tune the ftring.

19 O let not my inhuman foes rejoice,
Nor mock my mis'ries with infulting voice;
Nor feem by their deriding leers to boaft,
That I thy favour and thy love have loft. 60

20 For peace they hate, with impious malice fraught,
Dire ftrife employs their tongue, and fills their thought;
And with their curft devices they confpire
'Gainft men of gentle mind, that peace defire;

21 At me loll out their tongues, and, flouting, fay: 65
" Our eyes at length behold th' expected day."

22 This haft thou feen, O Lord; be ftill no more,
But fhield me, guard me, by thy gracious pow'r;

23 To judgment now, O mighty God, awake;
Stir up thy vengeance, nor my caufe forfake: 70

24 I to thy righteous juftice make appeal;
Stop their proud boafts; their ill-tim'd triumphs quell:

25 No more let their big hearts infulting cry;
" He falls at length, and ours the victory:"

26 But fince they made my miferies their boaft, 75
In dire oblivion let their names be loft;
Since they, invet'rate, my perdition fought,
Bring all their hopes, their flatt'ring views to nought.

27 While thofe dear fouls, that wifh'd my caufe fuccefs,
Sincere delight, fublimeft joy poffefs; 80
Thy great beneficence, thy juftice praife,
And fing thy glory in harmonious lays;

28 Then fhall my tongue thy righteous pow'r difplay,
And hymn thy honour'd name the live-long day.

P S A L M *XXXVI.*

1 CURST with deceitful joy his fottifh heart,
   His foul with fancied happinefs alert,
His flagrant guilt againft the wicked cries ;
There is no fear of God before his eyes.

2 With foothing plea and artful argument   5
He lulls his confcience to a falfe content ;
In vain-----his crimes are of the blackeft die,
And call for dreadful vengeance from on high.

3 For lo ! his tongue is tipt with frauds and lies,
Him to deceive, who on his faith relies ;   10
In wordly craft he chufes to excel,
And with celeftial wifdom fhuns to dwell.

4 Averfe to goodnefs is his headftrong will,
E'en on his downy bed he ftudies ill ;
With eyes afkance the paths of virtue views,   15
" And 'gainft his *better* mind the *worfe* purfues.

5 While thy great mercy, Lord, the heav'ns above,
And all thy works, and all thy creatures prove.

6 For higher than the higheft hills, does fhow
Thy goodnefs-----deeper, than the depths below. 20
Thy goodnefs, which the fons of men fuftains,
And all the beafts that range the wilds and plains.

7 Who can thy great beneficence exprefs,
The various gifts with which thy mercies blefs ?
E'en while with gratitude thy love he fings,   25
Man refts beneath the fhadow of thy wings.

8 On him thou namelefs bounties doft beftow ;
To him the rivers of thy pleafures flow ;

9 From thee life's fountain fprings ; from thee a ray
The mind illumes, and fpreads eternal day.   30

10 O ftill the bleffings of thy love impart
To all that ferve thee with a perfect heart ;

11 Me from th' infulting heel of pride defend ;
'Gainft the deftroying hand affiftance lend ;

12 Soon let them feel the vengeance of thy pow'r, 35
And fall fo low, that they may rife no more.

P S A L M *XXXVII.*

1 WHEN impious men in wordly fplendor live,
   And all the good poffefs that earth can give,
Scorn thou to murmur at their empty joy,
Nor envy what a moment may deftroy.

For

2 For foon their boafted riches melt away,　　　　　5
　Falfe are their pleafures, and their hopes decay;
　Like the green grafs, whofe bloom attracts our eyes;
　Cut by the cruel fcythe, it's verdure dies.

3 No; rather thou upon thy God depend;
　Him by a courfe of virtue make thy friend;　　　10
　So thou the bounties of his earth fhalt fhare,
　And feel the bleffings of a father's care.

4 With love of him thy fervent foul infpire,
　And he fhall fill thee with thy heart's defire.

5 To him thy fortunes and thy life commit;　　　15
　Soon fhalt thou find the glorious benefit;

6 Bright as the fun he'll make thy merit fhine,
　And on thy virtues beam a light divine.

7 Reft then on him, and with due patience wait,
　Nor at the joyous hours of finners fret;　　　20

8 Thine anger bridle, and thy wrath reftrain;
　O'er all thy paffions hold a fteady rein:

9 Soon droop the wicked; fuddenly they die,
　While righteous fouls fubftantial good enjoy.

10 Stay but awhile; the wicked is no more;　　　25
　In vain his habitation thou'lt explore;
　A defart now, his palace, late fo fair;
　Without a name he dies, without an heir.

11 Not fo the meek-----the earth fhall long be theirs,
　And when they die, they leave it to their heirs.　　　30

12 T' enfnare the good, is all the villain's joy,
　Pleas'd, if he guiltlefs merit can deftroy:

13 But heav'n, who knows, how fhort-liv'd is his pride,
　Does all his wily cruelty deride.

14 T' affail the poor, the wicked draws his fword;　　　35
　The poor, the happy fav'rites of the Lord;
　He bends his bow, the innocent to flay,
　T' extirpate thofe, who heav'n's high will obey.

15 In vain-----in his own bowels fheath'd his fword,
　Defends his favour'd poor th' almighty Lord;　　　40
　Broke is his bow; his arrows fruitlefs fly,
　While on their God, infur'd, the good rely.

18 Yes; long they flourifh, and, tho' *little's* theirs,
　That *little* they enjoy, devoid of fears;
　That *little* furnifhes fincerer blifs,　　　45
　Than all that profp'rous finners can poffefs.

17 For, while the pow'r of impious finners fail,
　Supported by their God, the good prevail;

Their

18 Their God, that promiſes a length of days,
   To ſpend in health, in happineſs, in peace ;   50
   That promiſes a num'rous progeny,
   To leave their ſubſtance to, whene'er they die :
19 Their God, that, when diſeaſes rage around,
   Their great protector from th' infection's found ;
   That, when the trumpet ſounds the dread alarm ;   55
   Preſerves them by his providence from harm.
20 But not the wicked thus receive his aid ;
   In times like theſe, his vengeance ſtrikes them dead ;
   Like fat of victims that expires in fume,
   Shall they in his tremendous wrath conſume.   60
21 The wicked borrows, tho' he never pays,
   Not ſo the juſt ; the fainting ſoul he'll eaſe ;
   To painful poverty aſſiſtance gives,
   And all the anguiſh of their hearts relieves.
22 Therefore his friends, 'cauſe he ſo freely gave,   65
   Their ſubſtance to his progeny ſhall leave ;
   While rot the wicked with the curſe of all,
   And his whole crimes upon his off-ſpring fall.
23 For God the good man loves, and guides his ſteps,
24 And with his hand ſupports him, if he flips.   70
25 Young have I been, and now, tho' grown in years,
   Still my hoar age my mem'ry not impairs ;
   And ne'er knew I the good man wanting aid
   And ne'er heard I his children beg their bread.
26 For, as he ever gave, and ever lent,   75
   Heav'n on his race continual bleſſings ſent.
27 Be virtue then thy aim, baſe folly ſhun,
   And thou a conſtant courſe of bliſs ſhalt run :
28 For love and equity the Godhead loves,
   And ne'er forſakes the virtues he approves :   80
   The good are ſtill preſerv'd in happy peace,
   While fail the wicked, and extinct their race.
29 Yes ; large poſſeſſions to the righteous fall,
   And to his children he preſerves them all ;
30 For why ; his mouth with heav'nly wiſdom glows,   85
   With truth, with juſtice, ev'ry period flows ;
31 The law of God is written on his heart ;
   He from it's ſacred dictates ſcorns to part ;
32 And tho' the wicked waits in ambuſcade,
   His life t' enſnare, his property t' invade,   90
33 Yet ſtill th' almighty Lord will be his friend,
   Will 'fore the judge his guiltleſs ſoul defend.

Wait

34 Wait then upon thy God; obey his laws,
And he for ever will support thy cause;
The Land he'll give thee ever to possess,
While soon the foes to truth, to virtue, cease. 95

35 As lifts the laurel high it's lofty head;
As with gay pride it's verdant branches spread;
The wicked thus I've seen exalted high;
Have heard him boast his pow'r, his God defy. 100

36 But soon his empty glories past away,
The vain, the idle *pageant* of a day;
Again to view him, oft I look'd around,
And not a trace of all his pride I found.

37 But mark the righteous in his constant race, 105
You'll find him live a good old age in peace.

38 While vile transgressors shall be soon destroy'd,
And all their base and impious schemes are void;

39 The righteous fix their safety in the Lord,
And he'll to them his certain aid afford: 110

40 To him when they apply, 'twill not be vain;
Them in their varied cares he'll long sustain;
From toils of artful men he'll keep them free,
And, 'cause they trust in him, their strength he'll be.

P S A L M XXXVIII.

1 ME, Lord, not in thy dreadful wrath, correct,
Nor let thy sore displeasure take effect.

2 Deep in my bones thy fatal arrows stand,
And much I'm wounded by thy heavy hand:

3 My anguish'd body feels thy deadly wrath, 5
And my whole system threatens me with death.

4 In all my guilt o'er-whelm'd, I quite despair;
Ah! load too heavy for my soul to bear!

5 O fatal folly! rankle now again
My wounds, their stench more grievous than their pain. 10

6 I droop, I totter, with my misery,
And all the day with killing anguish sigh.

7 With foul, with loathsome ulcers blister'd o'er,
No part have I but festers with a sore.

8 Quite weak, quite feeble with my pains I'm grown, 15
And my afflicted heart makes piteous moan.

9 Thou know'st the secret wishes of my heart;
A witness to her bitter groans thou art:

10 Deeply she groans-----my strength all from me flies,
And, lost in dreary darkness, stream my eyes. 20

My

11 My wonted friends, my kinfmen, ftand aloof;
   My filthy, fetid ulcers keep them off;
12 While to entrap my tortur'd foul, prepare
   My cruel foes, and lay for me the fnare.
13 But I, as dumb my tongue, as deaf my ear,   25
   For grief was filent, nor wou'd feem to hear :
14 Thus like a wretch quite ftupid, I became,
   That cou'd not clear, when they afpers'd, my fame.
15 In thee, O Lord, my only hope I place;
   My helplefs foul do thou, benignant, raife;   30
16 Let not my foes with infolence be gay,
   Nor proudly triumph, if I heedlefs ftray.
17 Still am I ready all thy ftripes to bear;
   To me well-known thy chaft'ning mercies are;
18 And well have I deferv'd-----I own my fin,   35
   And mourn the vile offender I have been.
19 But ftill my foes are in their numbers ftrong,
   Daily encreafe, and ftill add wrong to wrong;
20 Full hard they prefs me, and my life purfue,
   And are my foes, 'caufe to my God I'm true.   40
21 Forfake me not, O Lord; thy fervant free;
22 Make hafte to help me; I've no help but thee.

P S A L M *XXXIX.*

1 WHILE foes affail'd me round, I bravely faid,
      Not by the tongue I'd be to crime betray'd;
   My tongue to bridle, firmly I decreed,
   As by the bitted rein is rul'd the fteed.
2 Strict filence then I kept, tho' great the pain,   5
   And e'en from juft complaints did long refrain.
3 But as more fiercely burns the flame confin'd,
   With ftronger rage was fir'd my troubled mind;
   Thro' all reftraint at length my anguifh broke,
   And in thefe 'plaining terms to heav'n I fpoke :   10
4 " How long, O God, muft I endure the ftrife ?
  " What bounds are fet to this my wearied life ?
  " O tell the ftated number of my days;
  " When end my forrows; when begins my peace ?
  " When wings my foul to heav'n ? when leaves behind 15
  " This houfe of clay, ah! too, too long confin'd ?
5 " A very fpan is life, compar'd with thee;
  " Our years weigh nothing with eternity;
  " Swift as an empty fhade, they fleet away,
  " And our beft ftate's the *phantom* of a day.   20
                                  " Our

6 " Our blooming hopes one sudden blast destroys,
   " Pall'd are our pleasures, transient are our joys;
   " Vain all our cares, and all our labours vain,
   " With tedious toil our shining stores we gain,
   " Heap up our wealth, to leave it, when we're gone,   25
   " To whom?-----to heirs alas! to us unknown.
7 " Where then, O gracious God, shall I apply?
   " To thee, O Lord; I on thy pow'r rely.
8 " O free me from th' occasion of my woes,
   " My wicked crimes, from whence my evils rose;   30
   " Nor leave me in my miseries forlorn,
   " To fools, to sinners, a reproach, a scorn.
9 " When griefs surrounded me, I silence kept;
   " Spoke not my 'plainings, but in secret wept;
   " For them the punishments of sin I knew,   35
   " The woes that to my countless crimes were due.
10 " But now, O Lord, the bitter stroke remove;
   " Too weak to bear the killing pang I prove.
11 " Dost thou the wicked for their sins chastise?
   " Fails all their strength, and all their beauty dies;   40
   " Like garments fretted by the moth away,
   " They fade, they pine, they wither, they decay.
12 " Then pitying hear, all-clement God, my cry,
   " Nor from my pleading tears avert thy eye:
   " A stranger here, a sojourner I am;   45
   " As strangers, hither all my fathers came;
   " Had here no certain, no abiding place;
   " But ran a short, a momentary race.
13 " Yet spare me still awhile; thy hand restrain;
   " Let my tir'd soul some little respite gain,   50
   " Her strength retrieve, recruit her languid pow'r,
   " 'Fore I go hence, and shall be seen no more."

P S A L M XL.

1   WHEN swelling foes, elated with their pride,
      My ruin threat'ned, and my God defied,
Yet were my spirits gay; I fear'd no ill,
For well I knew, his eye wak'd o'er me still.
2 And soon was I with his deliv'rance blest;   5
Me on a rock of safety soon he plac'd;
Soon from the dreary pit, the miry clay,
My feet he rescued, and prepar'd my way.
3 Nay more; he taught me a new song of praise,
    In strains before unsung my voice to raise;   10
         G   In

In ftrains fo ftrong, fo fweet, that all who hear,
In him fhall place their truft, and him fhall fear.

4 And happy he, who in the Lord fhall truft,
Who braves the threat'nings of imperious duft ;
Who on no falfe infidious fcheme relies,   15
And 'fcorns to turn afide to fraudful lies !

5 Great is the love our God to man has fhewn ;
Many the gracious wonders he has done ;
The tongue the countlefs number can't declare ;
The mind their vaft *idea* ne'er can bear.   20

6 Such condefcenfion, fay, what tongue can tell,
When thou the awful fecret didft reveal ;
That not in facrifice was thy delight,
That thou the victims for our fins didft flight.

7 Then faid I ; " Lo ! I come, I come, prepar'd   25
" To do what thou thy high will haft declar'd ;
" I come, the folemn myftery to unfold,
" Which in thy facred volumes is foretold."

8 Yes, Lord, thy will I'll joyfully obey,
Thy will, my great delight, by night, by day ;   30
Writ on the faithful tablet of my heart,
Thy law I will perform in ev'ry part.

9 Conftant my lips thy wond'rous juftice tell,
And 'mong the pious tribes thy truth reveal :

10 Thy wond'rous juftice to myfelf alone   35
I've not confin'd-----to all, to all 'tis known ;
Thy wond'rous juftice all enraptur'd heard,
Of guilt, of virtue, thy diftinct reward.

11 Then let me, Lord, thy kind compaffion fhare ;
Thy goodnefs guard me with paternal care ;   40

12 For many are the ills my foul furround ;
My foul e'en her own frequent failings wound ;
My countlefs hair in number they exceed,
And make me with fevere repentance bleed.

13 But thou, good God, thy ftrong affiftance give ;   45
O hafte to aid me, and to bid me live.

14 Let fhame, let fure confufion them annoy,
Who feek my life by treach'ry to deftroy ;
Let dire difmay and bafe difhonour dwell
With thofe, who joy at my misfortunes feel :   50

15 Surrounded be they with diftrefs, with fear,
Who mock thy fervant, and his fufferings fneer.

16 But let all they, that love thy name, rejoice,
And to thy glory tune the grateful voice.

17 Poor tho' I am, tho' mifery is mine,　　　　　　　　　　. . 55
　Yet have I comfort in thy aid divine,
　Thou art my truft, my great fupport and ftay;
I Hafte, O my God, nor make too long delay.

P S A L M XLI.

1 **B**LEST is the man, who'll not the poor defpife,
　　But to his aid with fwift compaffion flies;
　Him with abundant mercy will repay
　Th' all-high, and chafe his forrows far away.
2 From foes, from perils he'll his foul defend,　　　　　　　5
　And grant him joys, that but with life will end,
　In peace, in opulence, he'll bid him live,
　And all the bleffings of his earth he'll give.
3 And when fome dire difeafe furrounds his head,
　When racking pains confine him to his bed,　　　　　　　10
　His bed he'll eafe, his fainting foul fuftain,
　To health reftore him, and drive off his pain.
4 For, when with violence of pain oppreft,
　I to my God this faithful pray'r addreft:
　" All-clement Lord, let me thy mercy feel,　　　　　　　15
　" My foul, with dire offences wounded, heal;
5 " Of unrepented fin I feel the force;
　" My foes with bitter imprecations curfe;
　" When fhall oblivion veil his name (they cry)
　" When will he breathe no more? when will he die?　　20
6 " And if they vifit me, and view my pain,
　" Grief in their clouded countenance they feign;
　" While inward joy dilates their villain-heart;
　" Which ftrait breaks out, when from my fide they part.
7 " In fecret, fee, th' invet'rate factions herd;　　　　　25
　" 'Gainft me they whifper flanders moft abfurd;
　" 'Gainft me with unrelenting hate confpire;
　" Big with proud hopes to compafs their defire.
8 " Now, when they fee me with my fuff'rings fpent,
　" Surely (they fay) from heav'n his pains are fent,　　30
　" Struck by the arrows of his God, he lies;
　" Shades him eternal night; he dies-----he dies.
9 " Nay; e'en my friend, who long my heart had known,
　" And made my table and my home his own,
　" 'Gainft me has with invet'rate malice rofe,　　　　　35
　" Ingrateful leaves me, and affifts my foes.
10 " But thou, O God, whom long I've made my hope,
　　" From my 'lorn bed, benignant, raife me up;
　　　　　　　G 2　　　　　　　　　　" Thy

" Thy love in my recovery difplay,
" That I their villain-hatred may repay."   40

11 Thus I implor'd, nor I implor'd in vain ;
Thou didft, O God, my finking foul fuftain ;
Me to my wonted health didft thou reftore,
And mad'ft my foes to give their triumphs o'er.

12 Frefh vigour to my frame didft thou impart,   45
Preferv'dft in innocence my drooping heart,
My fteps fupported'ft by thy hand divine,
And on thy *David* bad'ft thy prefence fhine.

13 For this great boon let *Ifrael's* God be prais'd,
Eternal altars to his name be rais'd ;   50
O'er all the fcatter'd nations let him reign ;
From age to age be bleft our God. *Amen*.

P S A L M *XLII.*

1   A S pants the hart to tafte the limpid flood,
     So longs my thirfty foul for thee, O God.

2 O fhall I ne'er behold the happy day,
When in thy houfe I fhall again be gay ?

3 No food but tears my weaken'd fyftem knows,   5
While ftill I bear the infults of my foes.

4 And yet this glad reflection fooths my mind,
In this bleft thought I confolation find ;
The time will come, when with the pious throng
Thy houfe I'll vifit, and make thee my fong ;   10
When there I fhall thy glorious works difplay,
And keep in folemn pomp the feftal day.

5 Why then, my foul, fo dreadfully difmay'd ?
Why thee fuch fad diftracting griefs invade ?
Difmifs thy fears, and on thy God rely ;   15
E'en yet fhalt thou return with victory ;
Yet with his pow'r thy caufe will he fupport,
And thou fhalt praife him in his awful court.

6 My joy, my only folace this, when I,
O *Jordan*, in thy forefts fkulking lie ;   20
When, *Hermon*, I thy rocky defarts trace,
And roam, an exile, with the beftial race.

7 What tho' misfortunes on misfortunes tread,
Tho' heav'n's dread terrors thunder o'er my head,
Tho' pours the rattling hail, the billows roar,   25
And the big founding waters dafh the fhore ;

8 If ftill, O God, thy mercies thou'lt difplay,
Soon will each low'ring cloud difperfe away.

Mean

Mean while, I'll in thy praise employ my tongue,
And now put up a pray'r, now chant a song;   30
By day, by night, me shall thy truth sustain;

9 My God I'll call thee, gently I'll complain;
With these expostulations sooth my woes;
   " Why am I made a *may-game* to my foes?
   " Why has my God forgot me? Will no more   35
   " Thy mercy aid, when prostrate I implore?

10 " Hear how with flouts my ears the impious wound;
   " How they their vile reproaches scatter round;
   " O hear them vent their blasphemies abroad,
   " And cry, insulting, Where is now thy God?"   40

11 But why, my soul, so dreadfully dismay'd?
Why thee such sad distracting griefs invade?
Dismiss thy fears, and on thy God rely;
E'en yet shalt thou return with victory;
Yet with his pow'r thy cause will he support,   45
And still thou'lt praise him in his sacred court.

P S A L M XLIII.

1 MY great avenger thou, O Lord, to thee
     Make I appeal against my enemy;
Against the fraudful, the deceitful man
Do thou, just God, my righteous cause maintain.

2 Thou art my surest hope, my strong defence;   5
Why have I not my wonted confidence?
Why do I fruitless mourn my sad distress?
Why with such fury do my foes oppress?

3 Beam forth thy light, thy kind assistance lend,
And 'gainst their fierce assaults my soul defend.   10
O lead me, lead me to thy holy hill,
Where downy peace, where heav'nly comforts dwell.

4 Then to thy altar I'll with transport go,
My heart with strongest gratitude shall glow;
My voice in hymns of harmony I'll raise,   15
And strike my lyre, to celebrate thy praise.

5 Why then, my soul, so dreadfully dismay'd?
Why thee such sad distracting griefs invade?
Dismiss thy fears, and on thy God rely;
E'en yet he'll crown thy brows with victory;   20
Yet with his pow'r thy cause will he support;
Thou still shalt praise him in his sacred court.

P S A L M *XLIV.*

1 THY glorious deeds, thy mercies,. Lord, of old,
    Our fathers oft their progeny have told ;
  Their fons with pious gratitude they've taught,
  What mighty wonders thou for them haft wrought.

2 How thou didft thy beneficence difplay,   5
  And drov'ft the nations from their feats away ;
  Didft the profaners of thy name deftroy,
  And badft thy people their domains enjoy.

3 For not their ftrength the mighty work perform'd ;
  Vainly without thy goodnefs they had arm'd ;   10
  They owe the conqueft, the fuccefs, to thee ;
  Thy dread right-hand beftow'd the victory.

4 Juftly thy tribes thy hallow'd courts attend ;
  Propitious hear them, and affiftance fend.

5 By thee alone fupported, we difmay   15
  The vaunting foe, and gain a glorious day ;
  By thee fupported, on their necks we'll tread,
  And fpurn them to the regions of the dead.

6 In our own bows no confidence we have,
  Nor fondly hope, that our own fwords can fave ;   20

7 But to thy conqu'ring arm our caufe commit,
  And in thy might our deadly foes defeat.

8 Therefore, while lafts this earth, thy praife we'll fing,
  And make our boaft of thee, all-pow'rful king.

9 But now thou'ft caft us off ; thou leav'ft us now ;   25
  No more the leader of our armies thou :

10 Now from the hoftile bands we fly away,
  Bafely we fly, and prove an eafy prey ;

11 Expos'd, like fheep devoted to be flain,
  We 'mid the nations rove for peace in vain.   30

12 Thou'ft of thy people made a public fale,
  Nor the low price does to thy wealth avail.

13 A fcorn unto our neighbours we are grown,
  Our griefs they laugh at, and they mock our moan.

14 A *bye-word* we're become-----they fhake the head----- 35

15 For this, confufion has my face o'er-fpread ;
  With fhame I glow, to hear their blafphemies,
  To fee, with what derifion they defpife.

17 All this is now our defpicable lot ;
  Yet we thy facred cov'nant ne'er forgot ;   40

18 Nay ; in our paths whatever dangers lay,
  Our fteady Feet have ne'er declin'd thy way ;

19 Tho' funk in deepeft woe, difgrac'd, forlorn,
By vileft foes infulted, tho' we mourn;
Tho' we a life of abject flav'ry breathe,   45
And tremble on the dreadful verge of death.

20 Had we, O Lord, thy fov'reign pow'r denied,
And on the aid of other Gods relied;

21 Sure thou hadft known it, fince to thee confeft
Stand forth the inmoft fecrets of the breaft: 50

22 And yet for thee we all thefe griefs fuftain,
And like the fatlings of the fold are flain.

23 Why flumb'reft thou, O Lord? Awake, awake,
And not for ever thy poor tribes forfake;

24 Why hid thy face? Why this fevere neglect?   55
Why our affliction wilt thou ftill forget?

25 With grief o'erburden'd, in the duft we lie,
Our weaken'd limbs their wonted aid deny;

26 Awake, awake; redeem us from our foes,
And let thy mercy diffipate our woes.   60

P S A L M XLV.

1   A GLORIOUS theme my raptur'd heart infpires,
        A theme the moft fublime my genius fires;
The king-----the king-----to him pertains the fong-----
The king infpires the lay, and fills my tongue.

2 The king, excelling all of mortal birth;   5
Far fairer than the faireft fons of earth;
What namelefs beauty! what majeftic grace!
What heav'nly radiance beams upon his face!
The king, to whom the pow'r, that all obey,
Eternal honours gives, eternal fway.   10

3 Approach, unconquer'd chief, and on thy thigh
Gird thy victorious fword, with majefty,

4 With glory bright-array'd; around thee fhine
Fair truth, ftern juftice, clemency divine;
Crown'd with bright conqueft thy refiftlefs hand,   15
Obey the nations round thy great command;

5 Pour dreadful vengeance on the ftubborn foe,
And let thy fatal arrows bring them low.

6 Thy fov'reign pow'r no time fhall bound, no fpace;
Not chang'd by years, not circumfcrib'd by place;   20

7 On juftice founded, 'twill for ever laft;
No force fhall harm it, no attempts fhall blaft.
The glorious ruler of the realms above
(O bleft indulgence of almighty love)!

Above

Above thy fellows high exalts thy name ;　　　　25
The facred oils adown thy veftments ftream ;　:
8 Thy veftments, o'er thy graceful fhoulders fpread,
Their odorif'rous fcents around thee fhed ;
Of *eaftern Caffia* the admir'd perfume,
Of *myrrhe* the tears, of *Alóés* the gum.　　30
9 But what bright blooming maids around attend,
That from a long imperial race defcend ?
Around thy queen fubmiffively they wait,
Thy queen, at thy right-hand who fits in ftate ;
Thy queen, with *Ophir*'s fpark'ling gold array'd,　35
With glittering gems adorn'd her glorious head.
10 And thou, fair confort, liften to the lay ;
Thy gentle foul let my fweet numbers fway ;
Thy royal father and thy natal feat,
Thy dear, thy weeping relatives forget ;　　40
11 Look on thy prince, thy prince revere, who lives
But on the joys thy heav'nly beauty gives :
12 To thee proud *Tyre* fhall her gay prefents fend ;
Thee fhall the noble and the great attend ;
Wait on thy nod, and bow with fuppliant knee ;　45
Pleas'd to receive a gracious fmile from thee.
13 Rich are the royal charmer's robes-----behold,
How bright fhe gliftens in her braided gold ;
With all their efforts' art and nature ftrove,
To make her worthy of a monarch's love.　　50
14 She comes ; the king receives the lovely prize,
And fpeechlefs tranfport lightens in his eyes.
Her maids attend her, maids divinely fair,
Whofe lovely forms their high defcent declare :
With fhouts of joy the people round them wait,　55
To hail their entrance in the palace-gate.
16 O high-born maid ! regret thy fire no more,
But view the pleafures of my regal pow'r ;
Let all thy beauties, let thy love be mine ;
I'll make thee mother of a royal line ;　　60
Thy fons fhall boaft a wide extended fway,
And diftant nations fhall their rule obey.
17 Thy beauties too, the fubject of my fong,
Shall ftill employ my lyre, and tune my tongue ;
Thy beauties late pofterity fhall fing,　　65
And blefs the lovely fair, that charm'd the king.

P S A L M

P S A L M *XLVI.*

1　OUR refuge and our strength is heav'n's high God;
　　Our certain aid, when troubles rage abroad;
2　Therefore why shou'd we fear, tho' dangers threat;
　　Tho' moves this solid earth from off her seat;
　　Tho' from it's basis starts each lofty hill;　　5
　　Tho' the stunn'd sea their tumbling ruins fill;
3　Tho' rise the waters, and the billows roar,
　　And the big waves insult the rocky shore?
4　For round the city, which th' all-high approves,
　　The sacred, solemn temple, that he loves,　　10
　　Streams a fair river, glad'ning, as it flows,
　　The blest inhabitants with sweet repose.
5　There, that no terrors may disturb their peace,
　　That she from hostile bands may rest at ease,
　　Dwells God himself, supports her with his aid;　　15
　　In vain the hostile bands her peace invade.
6　When rag'd the *heathen,* and prepar'd the war,
　　And struck the nations round with horrid fear,
　　From out his thunder spoke th' almighty Lord,
　　Trembled low earth, and melted at his word.　　20
7　For us the Lord of hosts displays his pow'r;
　　Our refuge he, whom *Jacob's* sons adore.
8　Come then, and see the wonders of his hand,
　　The workings of his pow'r in ev'ry land;
9　He bids the harrast world to be at peace;　　25
　　He bids the fury of the war to cease;
　　The bow he breaks, he snaps the deadly spear,
　　And stops the chariot in it's full career.
10　" Compose your troubled hearts to rest (he cries)
　　" And know the pow'r that in the Godhead lies;　　30
　　" I'm earth's sole Lord, and I'll support my claim,
　　" And all the nations shall adore my name."
11　For us the Lord of hosts displays his pow'r,
　　Our refuge he, whom *Jacob's* sons adore.

P S A L M *XLVII.*

1　CLAP your glad hands, ye people all, rejoice;
　　Shout to your God with loud triumphant voice;
2　The mighty God, tremendous in his wrath,
　　Whose boundless rule extends o'er all the earth:
3　Who 'as made the nations truckle to our sway,　　5
　　And e'en the pow'rful of the world obey:

H　　　　　　　　　　　　Who

4 Who 'as giv'n his chofen race a wide domain,
  And bleft them with a glorious, endlefs reign.
5 Hark! he comes forth; the chearful trumpets found;
  With fhouts the pious tribes attend around;   10
6 He comes, he comes; approach your God with praife,
  In hymns of joy your tuneful voices raife;
7 He comes, o'er all the univerfal king;
  Let heav'n's wide arch with acclamations ring;
  Ye fons of melody, fet forth his pow'r;   15
8 That e'en the *heathen* may their God adore;
  O'er all he rules, and from his lofty throne,
  Awful, he makes his righteous judgments known
9 To him the princes of the people fly,
  Own him their God, and on his aid rely;   20
  Own, that the heav'ns and earth and feas belong
  To him, and make omnipotence their fong.

P S A L M *XLVIII.*

1 GREAT is the Lord; moft worthy he of praife;
    Sing, fing his glory in melodious lays,
  Ye fons of *Sion,* where's the bleft abode,
  The radiant habitation of our God.
2 Of *Sion's* hill moft beauteous is the fite,   5
  Sion, the nation's joy, the earth's delight:
  Full to the north the king's bright manfions lie,
  And with refplendent beauty ftrike the eye.
3 There *Ifrael's* race have oft beheld the Lord
  Maintain their caufe, and pow'rful help afford.   10
4 With mad'ning rage the furious monarchs came,
  With fierce intent t' enwrap our walls in flame;
5 They view'd with wonder, trembled with difmay,
  And, ftruck with terror, haft'ned quick away;
6 Not greater terror ftrikes the matron's heart,   15
  When of approaching throes fhe dreads the fmart;
7 Not greater fears the heartlefs crew affail,
  When o'er the ftout-ribb'd fhip the waves prevail.
8 As to their fons our fathers oft have told
  Thy glorious deeds, thy miracles of old;   20
  So in the city of our God we've view'd,
  The fame bright fcheme of wonders ftill purfued;
  Still fhail our progeny on thee rely,
  Thou'lt ftill relieve, when in diftrefs they cry.
9 Thy gracious mercies, Lord, we'll ne'er forget,   25
  But 'fore thy altar gratefully repeat;

                                    Thy

10 Thy praife, thy juftice,, glorious as thy name,
　　To earth's extremeft bounds will we proclaim ;
11 Yes ; *Sion*'s hill to all the realms around,
　　Thy great, thy righteous judgments, fhall refound ;　　30
　　The fons of *Salem*, and her virgin train,
　　To endlefs time renew the grateful ftrain.
12 Walk round, ye faithful tribes ; her walls explore ;
　　Her ftrong, her lofty turrets, number o'er ;
13 Obferve her forts, her palaces, with care,　　35
　　And to your fons her wond'rous ftrength declare ;
14 That they may know, how mighty is the Lord,
　　What aids he'll to his chofen race afford ;
　　How he'll fupport them ever with his pow'r :
　　And, knowing, praife his name, till time's no more.　　40

P S A L M *XLIX.*

1 HOWE'ER difpers'd, ye various nations, hear,
　　　Ye fons of frailty, lend a lift'ning ear ;
2 Whether in honours and in wealth ye flow,
　　Whether immers'd in penury and woe :
3 Wifdom's the facred fubject of my fong,　　5
　　Wifdom employs my lyre and tunes my tongue ;
　　Wifdom, to all that hear her, fteady friend :
　　Plain is my parable, if you'll attend.
5 Why fhou'd the dread of diftant want controul
　　The active vigour of my heav'n-born foul ?　　10
　　Why forfeit I my claim to future blifs
　　By anxious cares for earthly happinefs ?
6 They, who in purple and in gold are dreft,
　　Of honours and of opulence poffeft,
　　With wealth, with pow'r elate, when dies the friend,　　15
　　Whom they with joy wou'd to the fhades attend ;
　　Him by their gold, their honours, can they fave,
　　Can they redeem him from the greedy grave ?
8 Ah no ; no wealth the parting foul can ftay,
　　That from the finking body fleets away.　　20
9 Inexorable death the bribe rejects ;
　　Nor pray'rs, nor tears, nor ranfom, he refpects ;
　　He views their proffer'd, gilded bait, with fcorn,
　　And bluntly tells them, there is no return.
10 The wife, the foolifh, feel alike his pow'r,　　25
　　While thanklefs heirs poffefs their fhining ftore :
11 Vainly they think, the lofty domes they raife,
　　Will fpread their honours e'en to after-days,

Their

Their large poſſeſſions will retain their name,
And fair-enrol them in the liſts of fame.　　　30
12 Alas! when once they die, when once no more,
Soon are forgot their name, their wealth, their pow'r.
13 Yet ſtill like folly to their race extends;
From family to family deſcends.
14 As the fierce wolf devours his fleecy prey,　　　35
Feeds on them death, and finiſhes their day;
And while bright hours, that never have an end,
And ſhining proſpects righteous ſouls attend;
Weak feeble age their beauty ſhall conſume,
And ſink their honours in the mould'ring tomb.　　　40
15 But me redeems my Saviour from the grave;
Me to himſelf, to glory, he'll receive:
16 Nor thou repine, when one of low eſtate,
By fortune favour'd, ſuddenly grows great.
17 What ſhall attend him, when he comes to die?　　　45
See, his unfaithful honours from him fly:
18 Tho', while he liv'd, he ev'ry good enjoy'd,
And flow'd in pleaſures, till his ſoul was cloy'd;
Tho' he to others ſhew'd the tempting way,
And bad them, like himſelf, be ever gay;　　　50
19 When to his fathers he deſcends below,
To thoſe black ſcenes of wretchedneſs and woe,
Where not one glad'ning ray his ſoul revives,
He then his mad prepoſt'rous folly grieves.
20 For man, of honours and of wealth poſſeſt,　　　55
If not with wiſdom's ſacred influence bleſt;
Not nobler than a beſtial can be thought,
And, like a beſtial, will at length be nought.

P S A L M *L.*

1 THE mighty God, whom heav'ns and earth obey,
Who bends the ſcept'red tyrants to his ſway,
Speaks his dread judgments to the nations round,
And hears the ſentence earth's extremeſt bound.
2 From *Sion*'s hill, in ſhining glory clad,　　　5
He ſpeaks, and fills the liſt'ning world with dread.
3 He comes; man's impious crimes he'll bear no more;
Before his preſence flames of fire devour;
No more a Saviour, he the judge aſſumes;
Tremendous winds ſurround him; lo! he comes.　　　10
4 Impartial in his proceſs, heav'n he'll call
With all her orbs, and this terreſtrial ball;

To

To witnefs to his juftice-----heav'n obeys ;
Earth owns, eternal truth his procefs fways.

5 " Ye pious tribes (he fays) with whom I've made   15
  " A facred covenant, be not difmay'd ;
  " With confidence approach ; 'difmifs your fears ;
  " Yon bright etherial arch your judgment hears ;
  " Your God himfelf is judge ; his juftice prove
  " Yon bright etherial orbs, that roll above.   20
7 " You firft I call, bleft *Abr'ham*'s favour'd race,
  " Whom long I've honour'd with peculiar grace ;
  " Yourfelves atteft beneficence divine,
  " And own that juftice, and that mercy's mine ;
8 " That few the victims, whofe attoning blood   25
  " In facred ftreams have on my altars flow'd ;
9 " I not reprove ; the fatlings of the fold,
  " The ftalled ox, indiff'rent, I behold ;
10 " Mine are the beafts that in the foreft rove ;
  " Mine are the beafts that range the hill and grove ;   30
11 " Where'er the favage beftials of the field
  " Retreat, their haunts are not from me conceal'd.
  " In the fteep rock, or on the lofty tree,
  " Tho' neft the feather'd tribes, they're known to me.
12 " If I, like man, the pangs of hunger feel,   35
  " Say, is it requifite, I thee fhou'd tell ?
  " Thy kind affiftance, fay, fhall I implore ;
  " I, who o'er all have univerfal pow'r ?
13 " Me will the flefh of bullocks fatisfy ?
  " The offer'd blood of fatted goats, drink I ?   40
14 " No, no ; the breaft with gratitude that glows,
  " The fervent heart that breathes it's honeft vows,
15 " My banquet thefe-----be thefe thy facrifice,
  " And when fevere diftrefs upon thee lies,
  " My name invoke ; thy drooping foul I'll raife,   45
  " And thou fhalt pay thy God with grateful praife."
16 But to the wicked fays th' almighty Lord ;
(The wicked hear, and tremble at his word)
  " Wretch ! wilt thou dare to plead my righteous laws,
  " My facred covenant, to fupport thy caufe ?   50
17 " Thou, who to hear inftruction didft refufe,
  " And with thy impious fcoffs my word abufe ?
18 " Thou with the thief, thyfelf a thief, didft join,
  " And mad'ft th' adult'rers filthy purpofe thine ;
19 " To mifchief prone, didft mifchief meditate,   55
  " And arm'dft thy villain-tongue with curft deceit :

                                       " Didft

20 " Didſt violáte of blood the ſacred ties,
　" And 'gainſt thy brother fram'dſt malicious lies :
21 " And, more t' enhance thy impious villainy,
　" 'Cauſe ſilent I, think'ſt I reſemble thee :　　　　　60
　" Vain is the thought-----thy crimes I'll now diſplay,
　" And ſet thy monſtrous deeds in open day.
22 " Ye liſtleſs crouds, that now your God forget,
　" Conſider this, and make a ſafe retreat ;
　" Leſt, when to judgment cited by my wrath,　　　65
　" Not one can ſave you from eternal death :
23 " And you, ye righteous, you your voices raiſe,
　" In ſongs of gratitude, in hymns of praiſe ;
　" This to eternal happineſs the road ;
　" This, this will place you nigh the throne of God.　　70

P S A L M *LI.*

1 　O　G O D of mercy, view my pleading tears,
　　　　And hear a contrite ſinner's earneſt pray'rs ;
2 My ſpotted ſoul from her defilements, clean ;
　O waſh me, cleanſe me, from my crying ſin ;
3 With ſhame, with anguiſh, I my crime confeſs ;　　5
　Abaſh'd, I own my horrid wickedneſs :
4 'Gainſt thee I've ſinn'd ; my monſtrous guilt thou view'ſt,
　And with immediate vengeance ſtrict purſueſt ;
　That man may own impartial juſtice thine,
　And curb their impious tongues 'gainſt pow'r divine.　　10
5 But ah ! remember, Lord, tho' great my blame,
　E'en from the womb my firſt infection came ;
　In ſin was I conceiv'd, in ſin brought forth,
　And came a vile offender from the birth.
6 While thou, a ſoul from all contagion free,　　15
　Doſt ſtill demand, rich in ſimplicity,
　A ſoul, with wiſdom arm'd, with innocence,
　A ſoul, unſpotted by the crimes of ſenſe.
7 Be thine the glorious work-----O let me ſhew
　Far purer in thy ſight than whiteſt ſnow.　　20
8 With peace, with joy, with gladneſs fill my mind,
　'Till my faint limbs their wonted vigour find ;
9 Let not thine eye my ſhocking guilt ſurvey,
　But waſh the filth of all my ſins away :
10 Cleanſe thou my heart, O God, from ev'ry ſtain,　　25
　Renew my ſoul that ſhe her health regain ;
11 And not in anger turn away thy face,
　But ſtill with thy enliv'ning ſpirit bleſs :

12 O still my hopes of happiness restore ;
   Uphold me still, that I may fall no more.   30
13 So shall transgressors, who thy mercy see,
   Forsake their errors, and give praise to thee :
14 O free me from the blood I basely spilt,
   O cleanse my soul from her enormous guilt:
   Then shall my tongue thy tender mercies sing,   35
   Thy righteous justice hymn, all-gracious king.
15 Ope then my lips, O Lord, and I will raise
   My grateful voice, to celebrate thy praise ;
16 The offer'd victim thou dost not demand ;
   The victim else shou'd 'fore thy altar stand :   40
17 Pleas'd with a nobler sacrifice thou art ;
   A broken spirit and a contrite heart.
18 Still *Sion*'s hill, still *Salem*'s walls defend ;
   Be still, O God, thy people's pow'rful friend ;
19 Then pure their off'rings, pure their hearts shall be,   45
   The chastest vows shall they put up to thee ;
   The fatted goat thy sacred fires shall feed,
   And the young bullock at thy altar bleed.

P S A L M LII.

1 WHY boast'st thou, tyrant, thy high crimes aloud ?
    Our God is ever to the righteous good :
2 Thy guileful tongue (a falshood ev'ry word)
   More fatal pierces, than the keenest sword ;
3 Mischief thou lov'st, and goodness dost despise,   5
   Truth hath thy hate ; thy dear amusement lies ;
4 A Slander, big with ruin, gives thee joy ;
5 Therefore th' avenging God shall thee destroy,
   Shall root thee out, that thou be seen no more,
   While man in vain thy dwelling shall explore.   10
6 This shall the righteous view with joyful fear ;
   Smile at thy punishment, and heav'n revere.
7 " Lo ! this the man (they'll cry) with impious pride
   " Who brav'd his maker, and his pow'r defied ;
   " Who his frail riches made his strength, and strove   15
   " By villain-arts to mate our Lord above !"
8 For me, I'll, like an olive, flourish long ;
   I'll in the mercies of my God be strong ;
   I in his house will dwell ; and night and day,
   The wonders of his mighty arm display ;   20
9 His glorious works, his clemency, proclaim,
   And hail for ever his tremendous name.

P S A L M

P S A L M *LIII.*

1 THE impious atheift, in his folly proud,
  At one almighty being laughs aloud :
Corrupt they're all ; from virtue's paths they turn,
And in the quenchlefs fires of luft they burn ;
Their fhocking crimes, their curft impieties,   5
Demand tremendous vengeance from the fkies.

2 Th' all-high looks down from his etherial throne,
To fee, if man his fov'reign pow'r will own ;
If yet the fons of earth accept his fway,
His name revere, and his dread will obey :   10

3 Ah no ! not one ; they 'gainft their God confpire,
Purfue the dictates of each wild defire,
In filthy fcenes of vice their hours employ,
And make their fhocking crimes their horrid joy.

4 Does then rank frenzy o'er the wicked reign, 15
That they fuch hideous blafphemy maintain ;
That they my people as their prey devour,
And, obftinate, reject almighty pow'r ?

5 Yet fure diftracting fears their hearts fhall wound,
And dread alarms their daftard fouls confound ; 20
For God fhall ftrike them with a fore difmay,
Shall break their bones, and fcatter them away,
With fhame his vengeance has their fteps befet,
And death and ruin all around them wait.

6 From *Sion*'s hill, O that the Lord wou'd fend 25
His fpeedy aid, and *Jacob*'s fons defend ;
Wou'd his own people from their bondage free,
And give them back their native liberty !
Then fhou'd the race of *Ifrael* fhout for joy,
And their glad tongues in grateful hymns employ. 30

P S A L M *LIV.*

1 SAVE me, my God ; protect me from the foe,
  That all may fear, thy name, thy pow'r may know ;
2 Lift to my pray'r ; O turn a gracious ear,
3 For ftrangers ftrike my heart with fudden fear ;
Againft my peace the fierce oppreffors rife ; 5
And have not fet thy vengeance 'fore their eyes.
4 But lo ! the Lord's my help ; he'll free my foul ;
He'll the vile fchemes of cruel men controul ;
5 By their own impious arts themfelves fhall fall,
And in the toils they've laid fhall perifh all. 10

Therefore

6 Therefore to him the folemn vow I'll pay,·
His praife I'll fing, his goodnefs I'll difplay;
7 For he from my diftrefs will fet me free,
And give fuccefs againft my enemy.

P S A L M LV.

1 MY earneft pray'r, O heav'nly father, hear,
　　　Nor on thy fuppliant fervant look fevere:
2 View with what forrows fwells my anguifh'd breaft;
What fatal griefs deny my foul her reft;
3 'Caufe of the malice of oppreffive foes,　　　　5
The bitter hate, with which they've 'gainft me rofe;
The killing flanders on my fame they caft,
Their caufelefs fury that will ever laft.
4 Pain'd is my heart, and forely weeps within;
My heart the horrors of the grave hath feen.　　10
5 A fudden *tremor* c..i my fyftem falls;
A fudden terror r..y fad foul appal!s;
6 'Twas then I faid; " Oh! cou'd I fly away,
" Cou'd to fome lone retreat myfelf convey;
" O cou'd I wing it like the plaintive dove?　　15
" Soon to the defarts, to the woods I'd rove;
8 " Swifter than winds I'd fkim the liquid air,
" Reach the wild wafte, and feek my folace there."
9 Deftroy them, Lord; confound each villain-tongue,
For range the city violence and wrong;　　　　20
10 Or night or day their mifchiefs never fail;
Their monftrous crimes in ev'ry ftreet prevail;
11 Within her walls each horrid guilt is found;
Rage, av'rice, fraud, deceit, and luft, abound.
12 Had fprung my mis'ries from an open foe,　　　25
I fhou'd expect, and ward againft the blow;
Or if fome mighty tyrant had affail'd,
Myfelf I 'ad 'galnft his violence conceal'd:
13 But fay, cou'd I my guardlefs foul defend,
When thus affaulted by my bofom friend?　　　30
14 One fo belov'd, I ne'er cou'd from him part,
But fhar'd with him the fecrets of my heart;
With him in focial converfe fpent the day,
With him thy temple fought, my vows to pay.
15 Let them no more their horrid mifchiefs breathe;　35
O fink them, fink them, in eternal death;
Monfters of iniquity from their birth!
Pour, heav'n, thy terrors; overwhelm them, earth!

I　　　　　　　　　　　　　While

16 While I my God invoke, to end my grief;
    While from his mercy I receive relief;   40
17 At morn, at even, while his name I praife,
    And fing protecting pow'r in grateful lays.
18 Yes; thou fhalt give me fafety in the war;
    In vain their num'rous bands fhall they prepare;
    In vain fhall threaten; I'll in thee be bold,   45
    The wonderful, th' almighty God of old:
    No longer fhall they boaft their cruel pow'r;
    Their proud relentlefs hearts fhall rage no móre.
20 Peace they'll pretend, yet fuddenly invade,
    Nor heed the folemn treaties they have made;   50
21 Smoother than milk, than oil, flows ev'ry word,
    Yet wounds more deeply than the keeneft fword.
22 But God my hope, my foul will he fuftain;
    On him the righteous ne'er rely in vain;
23 He'll on the wicked dire deftruction pour,   55
    Them in their youth fhall fudden death devour;
    Their fouls of half their days fhall he deprive;
    While a long round of years the righteous live.

P S A L M *LVI.*

1 L O! how my reftlefs foes my life purfue!
       With pity, Lord, th' impending peril view;
2 Many are they, my ruin that defire,
    And, infolently proud, my death confpire.
3 But, whate'er terrors compafs round my heart,   5
    Thou, thou alone my great protector art.
4 Thee will I praife, O God, on thee rely,
    And all attempts of mortal rage defy;
5 Yet conftant they detract from what I fpeak,
    And, to diftrefs me, villainoufly feek;   10
6 To fecret places they in crouds retreat,
    And there t' enfnare my guilelefs foul they wait.
7 Shall they efcape, and in their crimes go on?
    Rife in thy fearful wrath, and caft them down.
8 My toils thou numb'reft, and thou view'ft my flight;   15
    In thy fair tablet all my tears are writ:
9 Affur'd I am, that when to thee I cry,
    Thou wilt affift me, and my foes will fly;
10 Thee will I praife, O God; in thee I'll truft,
    And brave the threat'nings of imperious duft;   20
12 Sav'd by thy hand from my deftructive foes,
    Thee will I praife, to thee I'll pay my vows;

For

13 For thou'lt preferve me from the dreary grave,
My tott'ring feet, that they not flip, thou'lt fave;
Favour'd by thee, long life fhall I enjoy;　　25
Long to thy glory I'll that life employ.

P S A L M *LVII.*

1 TO thee, good God, I ev'ry bleffing owe;
　　O hear me now; thy wonted mercy fhew:
Beneath the fhelter of thy wings I'll reft,
Till all thefe dreadful ills are overpaft.

2 Thee I'll invoke, thy gracious aid implore,　　5
For ne'er was yet with-held thy faving pow'r.

3 From heav'n fhalt thou thy kind affiftance fend;
Me fhall thy mercy and thy truth defend;
Fruitlefs, my foes their impious flanders dart;
Fruitlefs they aim their mifchiefs at my heart:　　10

4 E'en tho' 'mong favage lions, fierce and fell,
'Mongft rav'nous beafts, that vomit fire, I dwell,
Whofe tongues than keeneft fwords more fatal are,
Whofe teeth wound deeper than the pointed fpear.

5 Do thou, O God, exalt thy glory high;　　15
Shew to th' aftonifh'd earth thy majefty.

6 For me their villain-toils they now prepare,
My poor afflicted foul they feek t' enfnare;
For me they've made a pit-----in vain they've made;
To the fame pit they are themfelves betray'd.　　20

7 Fix'd is my heart; my heart's refolv'd, O God,
To fpread thy praifes and thy name abroad;

8 Awake, my lyre-----my pfaltery-----my voice-----
At early dawn I'll in my God rejoice;

9 My fong of thee the nations round fhall hear;　　25
Struck with the theme, thy pow'r fhall they revere;

10 For to yon tracklefs clouds, yon heav'ns above,
Extend thy truth, thy clemency, thy love.

11 Do thou, O God, exalt thy glory high;
Beam on the wond'ring world thy majefty.　　30

P S A L M *LVIII.*

1 YE fages, plac'd on judgment's awful feat,
　　Say, is your procefs juft, without deceit?

2 Ah no! your hearts in villain-fchemes are ftrong,
And with the fhew of equity you wrong.
I 2　　　　　　　　　　　　　　E'en

3 E'en from your infant-years from truth you ſtray'd,　　'5
　And the vile dictates of your hearts obey'd.
4 Beneath your tongues a deadly poiſon lies,
　Your ears you ſtop, when heav'nly wiſdom cries,
　So the ſly aſp, when muſic gives th' alarm,
　Fears, 'tis the magic of ſome pow'rful charm.　　10
6 But thou their teeth, O ſov'reign ruler, bruize;
　Thy juſtice ſure the ſavage race purſues;
7 They bend the bow, the guiltleſs to deſtroy;
　O break their ſhafts, or let them fruitleſs fly.
　As 'mid the pebbles flows the ſtream away,　　15
　So with a ſwift deſtruction vaniſh they:
8 Yes; let them melt, as melts the ſlow-pac'd ſnail;
　Let death's grim horrid pow'r their ſouls aſſail;
　Yes; vaniſh they like an abortive birth,
　And tread no more with haughty ſteps the earth.　　20
9 Nor let their off-ſpring long enjoy the day;
　But with thy whirlwinds ſweep them quick away;
　Let them the fury of thine anger bear,
　Ere crackling thorns evaporate in air.
10 The righteous ſhall thy awful vengeance ſee,　　25
　And own with joy thy glorious equity;
　He in their impious blood ſhall waſh his feet,
　And ſay, " The juſtice of our God is great;
11 " That he our actions not indiff'rent views,
　" But with ſtrict vengeance wicked man purſues;　　30
　" That he a life of ſanctity regards,
　" And with his choiceſt gifts that life rewards."

P S A L M *LIX.*

1 O SOV'REIGN father, view my ſtubborn foes;.
　　With what relentleſs hate they've 'gainſt me roſe;
2 Around the men of blood my life beſet:
　O hear, and ſhield me from the woes they threat;
3 Lo! to entrap me, they their toils have laid,　　5
　And e'en the mighty join their pow'rful aid;
　By me uninjur'd they their fury breathe,
　And with unbated malice work my death.
5 O Lord *Jehovah!* ſov'reign ruler, riſe,
　On their malicious efforts caſt thy eyes;　　10
　Theſe vile tranſgreſſors of thy ſtatutes chace,
　Nor plead thy mercy for the impious race.
6 From early dawn like rav'ning dogs they rage,
　Whoſe famiſh'd maws no rapine can aſſuage;

　　　　　　　　　　　　　　　　　And

And when the fun his daily tafk gives o'er,   15
They fright the peaceful city with their roar.

7 From their vile mouths they caft forth bitter words,
  Which wound more deeply than the keeneft fwords ;
For blood, for blood, they roam with open cry,
And thy omnifcience and thy pow'r defy.   20

8 But thou, O God, not leave me thus forlorn ;
Thou view'ft their mad impieties with fcorn ;

9 My ftrong defence art thou, when foes invade,
And, patient, will I wait thy mighty aid.

10 Thou wilt prevent me with thy kind relief ;   25
Thy pow'rful hand will diffipate my grief ;
And, while thou fhalt my ceafelefs foes deftroy,
My grateful heart fhall glow with honeft joy.

11 Yet, Lord, our fhield, yet flay them not, left we
Forget the gratitude we owe to thee ;   30
But bring their proud, their cruel fpirits, down,
And let them wander in a land unknown.

12 And 'caufe their virulent, invenom'd tongues,
Were fill'd with falfhoods and with killing wrongs,
'Caufe with their horrid oaths they thee defied,   35
Enfnare them, Lord, in their enormous pride.

13 Confume them, O confume them, in thy wrath,
Root out their race, and ftrike them all with death ;
That the wide earth may know that *Jacob*'s God
The juft avenger of the righteous ftood.   40

14 Or, like to rav'ning dogs, from early dawn
Around the city let them roam, forlorn ;
And when the fun his daily tafk gives o'er,
For want of food in horrid anguifh roar.

15 Yet let them roam, and let them roar in vain ;   45
Nor one poor morfel to relieve them gain :

16 While I thy wond'rous pow'r will fing aloud,
At morn will fing the mercies of my God ;
My God, that made my cruel foes to ceafe,
My God, who gave me ftrength and gave me peace.   50

P S A L M LX.

1 OFFENDED with our crimes, O holy God,
    Thou'ft caft us off, and fcatter'd us abroad ;
Yet ftill thy juft difpleafure, Lord, reftrain,
And turn thee to thy chofen race again.

2 Lo ! thro' thine anger quakes our earth with fear------   5
Opes with difmay-----her fecret ftores appear-----

Clofe

Clofe up her wounds, her dreadful *tremors* ftay,
Confirm her bafe, and all our fears allay :
3 In fad, in wild aftonifhment we fink,
  And of thy bitt'reft indignation drink.   10
4 But lo ! the Lord hath heard-----he'll give his aid ;
  See his bright banners in the heav'ns difplay'd ;
5 The pious fouls that worfhip him, to free ;
  To give them from their terrors liberty.
6 Gracious he fpeaks, and holy are his words ;   15
  (What heav'nly joy his awful voice affords ?)
  " Fair *Shechem*'s fertile fields thy lot fhall be ;
  " I'll mete out *Succoth*'s lovely vales for thee.
7 " The faithful tribes of *Ifrael*, ar'n't they mine,
  " To me confirm'd by fanctions moft divine ?   20
8 " Therefore their fure protector I'll be found ;
  " Therefore for them I'll curb the nations round ;
  " I'll lay them all beneath their conqu'ring feet ;
  " *Idume, Moab, Palefline,* fubmit !"
9 Who to yon lofty town the way will fhew ?   25
  To *Edom*'s tow'ring gates our leader who ?
10 Say, wilt not thou, O God, tho" in thy wrath
  Thou'ft caft us off, and menac'd us with death ?
  Say, wilt not thou, tho' late thine anger rofe,
  And thou not lead'ft us 'gainft our haughty foes ?   30
11 But now, dread father, thy affiftance give,
  For vain are human aids, and but deceive :
12 Our leader thou, intrepidly we'll fight,
  We'll conquer and we'll triumph in thy might,
  Our leader thou, our haughty foes fhall bleed,   35
  And on their proftrate necks we'll joyous tread.

P S A L M *LXI.*

1 ALL-CLEMENT God, attend my earneft cry :
  2 In diftant lands tho' roam, an exile, I,
Thee in my heart's diftrefs will I invoke,
Thee will I make my ftrength, my fhield, my rock.
3 A fhelter moft fecure in thee I've found,   5
A firm fupport, when cruel foes furround.
4 Therefore beneath thy wings, affur'd, I'll reft,
And feek the temple with thy prefence bleft.
5 For thou my faithful vows haft conftant heard ;
For me a noble heritage prepar'd ;   10
To rule the nations who thy laws obey ;
To make them happy by my gentle fway.

                                       Thou

6 Thou to the king a length of days will give,
  Thou to a good old age shalt bid him live.
7 Long in thy house that he may suppliant stand,   15
  Reach forth thy blessings with a lib'ral hand.
8 Then free from danger, and devoid of fear,
  My grateful tongue thy mercies shall declare;
  To thee continual anthems I will sing,
  And hail the glorious God that guards the king.   20

P S A L M LXII.

1 **M**Y soul rests only on her mighty God;
    From him her safety and her strength has flow'd;
2 My rock of refuge he, my sure defence;
  Hence, ye vain fears; ye idle terrors, hence!
3 Ye sons of mischief, with weak malice fraught,   5
  How long will ye indulge each treach'rous thought!
  Soon shall ye be destroy'd; ye soon shall fall,
  And break to pieces, like a tumbling wall.
4 Vainly you all your empty efforts try,
  To ruin him whom God exalts on high;   10
  Vainly you false designing friendships feign;
  Vain are your lies; your imprecations vain.
5 Mean while, my soul, rest on thy mighty God;
  From him thy safety and thy strength hath flow'd;
6 Thy rock of refuge he, thy sure defence;   15
  Hence ye vain fears; ye idle terrors hence!
8 On him, ye people, constantly rely;
  Pour forth your hearts; he'll not the boon deny.
9 Surely the great, the proudest potentate,
  And the poor wretch that mourns his abject state,   20
  'Fore him are equal;-----weigh them in the scales
  With vanity, and vanity prevails.
10 Trust not in wealth, by violence obtain'd;
  'Twill go as fleetly, as 'twas basely gain'd;
  Riches flow in, but make them not your boast;   25
  Swiftly they wing away, and soon are lost.
11 Once God hath spoke, and twice I've heard him say,
  To him alone belongs eternal sway;
12 And I'll avow, and speak it all abroad,
  Justice and mercy both belong to God.   30

P S A L M

P S A L M · *LXIII.*

1 MY God, at early dawn to thee I'll cry;
    My soul's athirſt thy preſence to enjoy;
My weak, my languid fyſtem thee demands,
As aſk refreſhing ſhowers the parched lands:

2 Thy pow'r, thy radiant glory to behold,   5
Which in thy houſe thou wonteſt to unfold.

3 For ſweeter far than length of days to me,
Is thy ador'd, thy bleſt benignity.

4 Thee will I praiſe, while laſts this vital frame;
My grateful tongue ſhall eccho forth thy name.   10

5 Great the relief I from thy praiſe receive;
Not choiceſt cates ſuch ſweet refreſhment give.

6 At night I make thy tender love my ſong;
At morn thy mercies tune my raptur'd tongue.

7 For thou ſupport'ſt me ever with thy pow'r;   15
Beneath thy ſhelt'ring wings I reſt ſecure.

8 Thou art my ſoul's deſire, my heart's beſt love;
Thy ſtrong right-hand upholds me, as I move:

9 While they, who ſeek my ruin ſtrait ſhall go
Down to the diſmal, dreary ſhades below;   20

10 Soon ſhall they periſh by the fatal ſword,
Their lifeleſs limbs by rav'ning wolves devour'd.

11 But the glad king, and who their God revere,
Shall glory in the name by which they ſwear;
Shall boaſt the mighty Lord that they adore,   25
While fools in ſilence ſhall their guilt deplore.

P S A L M *LXIV.*

1 MY foes aſſault me with relentleſs hate;
    Hear me, my God; thy favour I intreat.

2 O ſave me from the vile inſidious ſnare,
The ſecret toils they 'gainſt my life prepare.

3 Their tongues are whetted like their pointed ſwords;   5
More deep, than arrows, wound their bitter words:

4 That at the juſt in ſecret they may aim,
And ſtrike, ſecure, the heart that's free from blame.

5 They, firm in miſchief, lay the private ſnare,
And, ſelf-encourag'd, laugh away their fear: 10

6 Miſchief their ev'ry thought, their ſole employ,
Miſchief they make their ſolace and their joy.

7 But not from thee can they their crimes conceal;
They ſoon the arrows of thy wrath ſhall feel;

They

8 They by their own envenom'd tongues fhall die----- 15
  With dread amaze fhall they, that view it, fly,
9 The juftice of an angry God fhall own,
  And make the terrors of thy vengeance known.
10 While righteous men, well-grounded in their hope,
  Shall give their faithful fouls their fulleft fcope, 20
  Still truft in thee, and glory in thy name,
  And hail their gracious God with loud acclaim.

P S A L M LXV.

1 IN *Sion's* facred fane the joyous lay
  Thy name attends ; thy favour'd people pay
The votive offering, Lord ; the hallow'd blood
Flows round thy altar in a purple flood.
2 Propitious, thou our faithful vows doft hear ; 5
  To thee fhall fly the fons of men in pray'r.
3 Thy punifhments for fin afflict me fore ;
  Cleanfe me, my God, and they fhall wound no more.
4 Bleft is the man, whom thou fhalt chufe a friend,
  And in thy facred temple bid attend ! 10
  O glorious lot ! O heavenly employ !
  Thy facred temple fills his foul with joy.
5 The nations tremble with a dread difmay,
  When thou thy righteous judgments doft difplay ;
  When fall thy terrors on the impious proud, 15
  When crown thy bright rewards the humbly good.
6 Great is thy pow'r----when fhatter'd by the ftorm,
  Thou bid'ft the mountain on her bafe ftand firm.
7 By winds difturb'd, thou ftill'ft the roaring fea,
  And doft the tumults of the world allay. 20
8 Thy thunder rolls, thy rapid lightnings glare ;
  The hearts of all are funk in awful fear :
  Thy fun breaks forth, and gives to nature birth ;
  Owns thy beneficence the quicken'd earth :
9 Thou pour'ft thy waters on the thirfty foil ; 25
  The fatten'd lands reward the ploughman's toil :
  With fruitful fhow'rs reviveft thou the fields,
  And the rich glebe it's golden produce yields :
10 Falls on the ftubborn earth thy pearly dew ;
  The plains in all their verdant pride we view : 30
11 Or on the ridgey hills, or in the vales,
  The glad'ning influence of thy pow'r prevails ;
12 Gaily the herds along thy paftures rove ;
  Climb the fteep cliff, or range the leafy grove ;

K
Where'er

Where'er they range, fair herbs and flow'rs abound;   35
Rich affluence covers the enamel'd ground;
Their God, the hills, the plains, the vallies sing,
And bless the bounties of their heav'nly king.

P S A L M *LXVI.*

1 YE scatter'd nations, sing in tuneful lays,
   · In loftiest strains, your great creator's praise;
2 Sing, sing the honours of his holy name,
   Extol his glory, and his pow'r proclaim.
3 With reverence say, " Thou sov'reign Lord of all,   5
   " Who mad'st yon heav'ns and this terrestrial ball,
   ". How dread thy pow'r ! beneath thy conqu'ring feet
   " Crouch thy proud foes, and to thy rule submit:
4 " To thee the earth shall pious homage pay,
   " Sing to thy name, thy glorious name display."   10
5 Approach, and hear the wonders of our God;
   With his stupendous works the world he aw'd;
6 He drove the waters from their oozy bed,
   And on firm ground his favour'd people led;
   With joy they view'd their God their feet sustain;   15
   With joy they walk'd as on a flow'ry plain.
7 O'er all, o'er all, he holds eternal sway,
   His eyes the nations of the earth survey;
   Hear this, ye wicked, and rebel no more,
   Lest you too late your wretched pride deplore.   20
8 Ye people, bless the great almighty Lord;
   By ev'ry nation be his name ador'd;
9 Our souls does he support; in him we live,
   From him protection in our paths receive.
10 For thou hast prov'd us, Lord; our hearts thou'st tried,   25
   As by the flame the silver's purified;
   Our feet hast hamper'd in th' insidious net,
   Our way with sore distresses hast beset.
12 The threat'ning tyrants gall'd us in their wrath;
   Thro' fires, thro' mad'ning floods, we' incounter'd death : 30
   Yet still thy mercy bad our sorrows cease;
   Again thou'st given us life, thou'st giv'n us peace.
13 Therefore I'll to thy temple suppliant go,
   And pay with gratitude the promis'd vow;
15 The bounding bullock, and the horned ram,   35
   The browsing goat, the young and guileless lamb.
16 Approach, attend, who your creator fear :
   To me his wond'rous goodness I'll declare;

                            Gracious

17 Gracious he heard, when proftrate I implor'd ;
   (And be the God that hears our pray'rs, ador'd):   40
18 The impious fouls, that not his name revere,
   Tho' loudly they invoke, he fcorns to hear :
19 'But me he heard, his mercy not denied,
   And gave immediate folace, when I cried :
20 Therefore, fince he my finking foul hath rais'd,   45
   His honour'd name eternally be prais'd.

P S A L M LXVII.

1 LORD, on thy people let thy mercy fbine,
     To us extend thy clemency divine ;
2 That to the world thy goodnefs may be known,
   That earth thy great beneficence may own ;
3 That thee the realms in joyous fongs adore,   5
   And hymning congregations chant thy pow'r.
4 Let ev'ry age exult with pious joy ;
   Their tongues in praife let all mankind employ ;
   For thou, of all the fov'reign judge, difplay'ft
   Thy righteous juftice, and with wifdom fway'ft.   10
5 Praife all thy glorious name, all-pow'rful king,
   And in fublimeft lays thy mercies fing ;
6 For thou fhalt glad our lands with rich increafe ;
   With corn, with oil, with wine, the plains thou'lt blefs ;
7 On the whole earth thy bounties thou fhalt pour,   15
   And all her fons with rev'rence fhall adore.

P S A L M LXVIII.

1 RISE, fov'reign Lord, in all thy terrors rife ;
    Lo ! vile impiety thy prefence flies ;
2 The wicked, lo ! thy prefence fly thro' fear,
   Like fmoke they vanifh into empty air ;
   Thy vengeance ftrikes them ; they with dread expire,   5
   And melt like wax diffolving in the fire.
3 Not fo the righteous ; fill'd with pious joy,
   In loud *hofannas* they their hours employ :
4 Sing, gracious God, thy great refiftlefs fway,
   And all the wonders of thy pow'r difplay ;   10
   How on thy heav'ns, in thy triumphal car,
   Thou rid'ft, fupported by the ambient air ;
5 How o'er ungrateful man thy cares extend,
   The *orphan's* father, and the widow's friend ;

K 2

How

6 How thou, ftill to fupply the human race,   15
   With a large iffue crown'ft the chafte embrace ;
   How, when the fetter'd captives fue to thee,
   Benign thou hear'ft, and giv'ft them liberty ;
   Doft curfe the ftubborn, the rebellious bands,
   With barren fields, with defolated lands.   20
7 When *Ifrael's* favour'd tribes, from bondage freed,
   Thro' the dry defart, gracious, thou didft lead;
8 Trembled low earth, aftonifh'd at thy pow'r ;
   The heav'ns above pour'd down their watery ftore ;
   E'en *Sinai's* top, at thy dread prefence ftruck,   25
   E'en *Sinai's* tow'ring top, with terror fhook.
9 Parch'd with the drought, when gape the thirfty plains,
   Thou pour'ft in plenteous fhow'rs thy fruitful rains ;
   By the glad fhow'rs refrefh'd, the teeming earth
   Opens her womb, and gives her produce birth ;   30
   See the rich fields with ripening herbage gay ;
   The lofty trees their various fruits difplay ;
   Thefe bleffings to thy chofen doft thou give,
   To that juft race, that in thy precepts live.
11 When threat'ning kings pour'd forth their num'rous bands, 35
   And ftruck with horrid fear the trembling lands,
   Spoke the high God ; his mandate ftrait obey'd
   The tott'ring matron, and the tim'rous maid.
12 The haughty tyrants vaunt their troops in vain ;
   They turn, they fly, they fall, they ftrew the plain ;   40
   The maids, the matrons, to the plunder hie,
   And blefs the God that gives the victory ;
   They hymn his glory in harmonious lays,
   And tune their harps to celebrate his praife.
13 Tho' mid the pots, in fmoke, in filth, ye lie,   45
   Ye ftill the dove in beauty fhall outvie ;
   The dove, whofe wings with pleafure you behold,
   With filver fpread, her feathers ting'd in gold.
14 Yes ; *Salem*, that alate in darknefs lay,
   (Vanquifh'd her pow'rful foes with dread difmay) :   50
   In fplendor rifes, far above her hope,
   And fhews more fair, than *Salmon's* fnowy top.
15 Let *Bafhan* boaft his head enwrapt in clouds,
   His fpacious forefts, and his fpreading woods ;
   Vainly it emulates that facred hill,   55
   Where heav'n's all-pow'rful Lord delights to dwell ;
17 E'en he, of human race the fire, the friend,
   Whom thoufand thoufand cherubims attend ;

                                                    Whom

Whom thousand thousand glitt'ring cars await;
Whether to *Sinai*'s height he rides in state;   60
Whether his presence does the temple grace,
To him up-rear'd by his peculiar race;
18 Whether, triumphant o'er rebellious foes,
Aloft to yon bright realms above he goes:
His stubborn foes in captive chains are led;   65
His conqu'ring arm, so late despis'd, they dread;
They own him now the universal king,
And to his hallow'd fane their victims bring.
19 Prais'd be the mercies of our sov'reign God,
Who 'as daily blessings on our lives bestow'd!   70
20 Our great salvation thou; in thee we breathe;
'Tis thou that giv'st, and savest us from, death;
21 Thou wound'st the rebel's head; by thee he dies;
With his black blood his vital spirit flies.
22 But to thy tribes blest mercy dost thou shew;   75
Safe thou protect'st them from the cruel foe;
Thou thro' the deep again wilt clear the way,
As erst thou lead'st us thro' the wond'ring sea;
23 That they their feet may dip in royal gore,
And e'en their dogs their carcases devour.   80
24 They, who with rev'rence to thy temple go,
The solemn triumphs of our God shall know;
25 Shall view the vocal choir, thy praise that sing,
That tune the harp, and strike the trembling string;
With raptur'd hearts shall hear the virgin-throng,   85
With their harmonious timbrels join the song.
26 In joyous shouts the glad assemblies rise,
And raise thy wond'rous glories to the skies:
27 The sons of *Benjamin* the concert join,
The noble youths of *Judah*'s royal line;   90
The valiant chiefs of *Zebulun* are there;
The chiefs of *Napthali*, renown'd in war:
28 Chiefs, who, with fortitude inspir'd by thee,
Fought bravely, and were crown'd with victory.
29 By them subdued, the kings around attend   95
Thy temple, and afore thy altar bend:
30 The hostile bands, that on their prowess stood,
The haughty chieftains, whose delight was blood,
Rebellious when they prov'd, didst thou submit,
And mad'st them lay their laurels at thy feet.   100
31 To thee their tribute *Egypt*'s princes pay,
And distant *Æthiopia* owns thy sway;

Thy

32 Thy praiſe the kingdoms of the earth ſhall ſing ;
   Yes ; hail, ye nations, your eternal king,
33 In heav'n who rules, with glory bright array'd,   105
   Whoſe mighty voice all nature hears with dread ;
34 Hail him, the God, who gives in war ſuccéſs ;
   Whoſe watchful cares o'er *Iſrael* never ceaſe ;
   Who is his people's firm ſupport and ſtay ;
   Whoſe pow'rful ſtrength yon low'ring clouds diſplay ;   110
   Whoſe preſence in his temple ſtrikes with fear ;
   ------Hail him, ye nations, and his name revere.

P S A L M *LXIX.*

1 BENIGN O hear me ; ſave me, gracious God ;
   Sinks my ſad ſoul in grief's o'erwhelming flood ;
2 In the deep mire my feet unfirmly tread ;
   The threat'ning billows compaſs round my head ;
3 My ſapleſs jaws are ſhrunk with conſtant cries ;   5
   Deny their wonted aid my weaken'd eyes ;
4 Far more in number than my countleſs hair,
   The foes that bear me ceaſeleſs hatred, are ;
   Each day in number ſtill theſe foes increaſe,
   And on my rights with ravenous hand they ſeize.   10
5 Thou know'ſt, O Lord, my innocence of heart ;
   A witneſs to my guileleſs ſoul thou art ;
6 Let not my woes affect the good with ſhame,
   Who know I'm wretched, 'cauſe I love thy name.
7 For thee I've borne this mis'ry, this diſgrace,   15
   For thee diſhonour overſpreads my face.
8 My brothers ſhun me, and my preſence fly
   My mother's ſons, as if an alien I.
9 With zeal I burn, to ſee thy hallow'd houſe
   Profan'd, to hear deſpis'd the ſolemn vows :   20
   From their vile mouths the blaſphemies that fall,
   With bitt'reſt anguiſh wring my tortur'd ſoul.
10 I weep, I faſt, or feed upon my tears,
   While they, inſulting, mock my pious cares ;
11 In humbling ſackcloth when my limbs are clad,   25
   A tale, a proverb, and a jeſt, I'm made :
12 The beggars at the gate my mis'ries flout,
   And I'm the *ſing-ſong* of the drunken rout.
13 But tho' thro' grief I feel a ſtrong decay,
   Thee ſtill, dread father, will I make my ſtay ;   30
   I'll on thy juſtice, on thy love depend,
   For thou art ever to the good a friend.

O

14. O free me, free me, from this miry clay.;
    O chace my causeless, cruel foes away;
15 My soul, from sinking in the waters, keep;   35.
    O save me from the horrors of the deep.
16 Hear me, my God; thy mercy's still the same,
    And in that mercy I protection claim.
17 On thee relying, I to thee have pray'd,
    Turn not thy face, but grant a timely aid: 40
18 Propitious come; redeem my sinking soul;
    The horrid counsels of my foes controul.
19 Thou know'st, O God, the infamy, the shame,
    From them I've suffer'd, 'cause I love thy name:
20 Griev'd my pain'd heart; yet none wou'd share my grief, 45
    No friend consol'd me, or wou'd give relief.
21 For food I ask'd; they mix'd with gall my meat;
    For drink, and *aconite* they 'fore me set;
22 O be their tables to themselves a snare;
    O turn their plans for peace to fatal war,   50
23 Darken their eyes, that they no longer see;
    Weak be their loins; their bodies languid be:
24 On them the fury of thine anger pour;
    Bear they thy vengeance, till they breathe no more;
25 Their homes with no inhabitant be blest,   55
    And in their tents let rav'ning bestials rest;
26 For they've insulted those who feel thy wrath;
    And with their taunts have wounded, worse than death;
27 Crime let them add to crime, that they mayn't know
    The blest effects that from thy mercy flow: 60
28 Their impious names let not life's volumes hold;
    And with the righteous be they not enroll'd.
29 But poor, afflicted, indigent am I;
    Raise me, O God, and set me safe on high;
30 Then I in honour of thy name will sing,   65
    And to thy glory fit the trembling string.
31 More grateful this, than if th' attoning blood
    Of horned victim on thy altar flow'd.
32 This shall the humble see with pious joy,
    And in glad praise their faithful hearts employ.   70
33 For hears the Lord the poor; he'll not despise
    His pray'r, who for his name in bondage sighs.
34 Praise him, O earth and seas and heav'ns above;
    And all in earth, in sea, in air, that move:
35 *Sion* he'll save, and *Judah*'s cities build   75
    So strong, that not to force, to time, they'll yield:

                              Her

36 .Her fertile lands his people fhall enjoy,
   And leave them to their off-fpring when they die ;
   Their off-fpring, who, like them, fhall long poffefs,
   While him they ferve, their rich domains in peace.   80

P S A L M *LXX.*

1 TO thee, in my diftrefs, I proftrate fall ;
    Bleft father, aid me, for on thee I call ;
2 Let fhame, let dire difhonour, them confound,
   Who by infidious fnares my foul wou'd wound ;
   When calls the trumpet's fprightly found to arms,   5
   Strike thou their hearts, O God, with dread alarms ;
3 That they may to their coward-terrors yield,
   Turn bafely back, and trembling fly the field.
4 While they, who truft in thee, thy laws who love,
   Their grateful fouls in joyous anthems prove,   10
   ·Thy mercies to the righteous magnify,
   And raife their maker's praifes to the fky.
5 Poor tho' I am, tho' mifery is mine ;
   Yet have I folace in thy aid divine ;
   My great deliverer thou ; my ftrength, my ftay ;   15
   O diffipate my griefs ; nor make delay.

P S A L M *LXXI.*

1 IN thee, all-clement God, my hopes I place ;
    O never let thy fervant know difgrace ;
2 But hear ; thy kind indulgent mercy fhew,
   And bid thy juftice free me from the foe :
3 My rock, my fortrefs, my falvation, thou ;   5
   Hope of my youth, and object of my vow,
   To thee I fly, as to a fure defence,
   To thee, bleft guardian of my innocence ;
   Caufe thou the fchemes of cruel men to fail ;
   Nor let their efforts 'gainft my peace prevail.   10
6 To me thy mercies have been always great ;
   Thofe mercies oft I gratefully repeat ;
   How from my birth thy goodnefs thou haft fhewn,
   How from my infant-years thou'ft led me on.
7 Now of derifion I an object prove ;   15
   Yet ftill my certain refuge is thy love ;
8 Therefore, while glads the radiant fun the day,
   Thine honour I, thy goodnefs will difplay.

Of

9 Of impious foes protect me from the rage,
  And not forſake me in my feeble age :   20
10 Conſtant their ſecret miſchiefs they prepare,
  And greatly hope, they ſhall my life enſnare :
11 " His God denies him aid ; he's ours (they cry)
  " Now ſeize him, take him, and the wretch deſtroy."
12 But thou, O God, thy kind aſſiſtance lend,   25
  Baffle their hopes, and my poor ſoul defend ;
13 With vile diſhonour and with ſhame meet they,
  To certain ruin who'd my ſteps betray ;
  Infatuate thou their ſchemes, their hearts confound,
  Who make it all their joy my ſoul to wound.   30
14 For in thy mercy I will ever hope,
  I'll praiſe the bounteous God that rais'd me up ;
15 Thy love unmerited I'll daily ſing,
  And to thy glorious name attune the ſtring ;
16 Extol the pow'r, that gives me ſtrength in war,   35
  And thy ſtrict juſtice faithfully declare.
17 My youth thou'ſt guided in the perfect road,
  Nor have I prov'd ungrateful to my God.
18 Now then, when age with all it's ills oppreſs,
  Now not deſert me in my deep diſtreſs ;   40
  That I to nations yet unborn may ſing
  The pow'r, the mercy, of my heav'nly king.
19 Thy juſtice, Lord, aſcends yon heav'ns above ;
  O dread creator, who like thee can prove ?
20 True ; thou didſt plunge me in the depths of grief,   45
  But ſoon thy mercy gave my ſoul relief :
21 Pow'r, wealth and honour, ſoon didſt thou ſupply,
  And gav'ſt me peace and happineſs t' enjoy.
22 Therefore my pſalt'ry and my harp diſplay
  Thy truth, O *Iſrael's* God, from day to day ;   50
23 Therefore my ſoul, by thee redeem'd from woe,
  In ardent praiſe her gratitude ſhall ſhew ;
24 Therefore thy righteous acts ſhall fill my tongue ;
  The juſtice of my God my conſtant ſong ;
  Who on my foes did dire deſtruction pour,   55
  My foes, who ſought his ſervant to devour.

P S A L M *LXXII.*

1 LET me, good God, my righteous ſuit obtain ;
  Impartial o'er my people let me reign ;
And for my ſon (O hear a father's pray'r)
Some portion of thy juſtice let him ſhare ;

L   By

2 By equal laws thy favour'd nations fway,   5
  Nor turn from pleading poverty away.
3 Then fhall the hills exalt their heads in peace;
  The woods and plains fhall heav'n-born juftice blefs.
4 With equity the injur'd let him hear,
  While hard oppreffors his refentment fear.   10
  Safe let the poor to his protection fly,
  Affur'd, that he'll immediate aid fupply:
5 That, while the beamy fun fhall gild the day,
  And the pale moon fhines forth with borrow'd ray,
  The ages yet to come may dread thy pow'r,   15
  Thy will revere, thy glorious name adore.
6 Down from above return the heav'n-born maid,
  And o'er the nations all her influence fhed;
  As from thy goodnefs falls the fleecy rain,
  And fpreads a glorious plenty o'er the plain.   20
7 His fceptre let the virtues all attend;
  Prove to the virtuous he a fteady friend;
  Long let them flourifh, while celeftial peace
  Their fouls with all her balmy fweets fhall blefs.
8 Extend his wide domains from fea to fea,   25
  While only earth's own bounds confine his fway.
9 Be his vaft *Æthiopia*'s defart land;
  Own all his foes fubmiffive his command;
  Bow at his awful feet, and grace implore,
  Their heads with humbling afbes cover'd o'er.   30
10 To him their gifts the world's high mafters bring,
  Tarfus' proud prince, *Arabia*'s haughty king;
  And all the monarchs of the ifles, whofe bounds
  Old ocean with his ftormy floods furrounds.
11 'Fore him fall all that have imperial fway;   35
  Him all the nations of the globe obey.
12 May he the wretched in their mis'ries aid,
13 And free the poor, when cruel foes invade;
14 From fraud, from violence, their fouls protect,
  And to their urgent plea have due refpect.   40
15 Crown'd with bright glory, long may he furvive,
  And *Sheba*'s yellow tribute long receive;
  For him his people long put up their pray'rs,
  And blefs the influence of his royal cares.
16 May e'en the defart hills their harvefts yield,   45
  (Their fterile tops with golden plenty fill'd)
  The tow'ring corn it's waving ears fhall fhew,
  As high on *Lebanon* the cedars bow;

                                   While

While o'er the city spreads a num'rous race,
As o'er the verdant plains the spiry grass. 50
17 Long may the glories of his name endure ;
His mem'ry last, till time itself's no more ;
His people, blest in him, as he in them,
Him equally their prince and father deem.
18 Praise, might and majesty, to Israel's God, 55
Who sheds his gracious bounties, all abroad ;
19 Eternal honours wait upon his name ;
Praise him, ye sons of men, with loud acclaim ;
O'er the wide world his glorious name be shewn,
And fall the nations prostrate 'fore his throne. 60

P S A L M LXXIII.

1 HIS mercies to the good will heav'n ensure,
    To all whose hands are clean, whose hearts are pure :
2 And yet how nigh I 'ad from my duty stray'd,
When I the counsels of his wisdom weigh'd ?
3 Mad was my heart, when I the wicked saw, 5
Who made their impious wills their only law ;
When I beheld them of their pow'r possest,
With health, with peace, with prosp'rous fortunes blest.
4 Vig'rous and strong, the paths of life they tread,
Fear not mischance, nor death's grim horrors dread. 10
5 The anxious cares that other men depress,
The killing griefs that righteous souls distress,
Are never theirs ; in happy ease they live,
Flow in their joys, and have not learn'd to grieve.
6 Therefore with insolence, with pride they swell, 15
No pangs for injur'd innocence they feel,
But violence and rapine make their joy,
And call it wond'rous glory, to destroy.
7 Fill'd are their garners, countless is their store ;
Yet their insatiate souls still thirst for more : 20
More still they have-----how fair their lots are cast !
More than their wanton luxury can waste.
8 Corrupt their hearts, oppression's all their thought ;
With vast ideas of themselves they're fraught ;
Proud is their speech, and lofty are their eyes ; 25
9 Still higher in their monstrous guilt they rise ;
Not with their insults on the world content,
'Gainst heav'n's high Lord their blasphemies they vent.
10 With souls astonish'd this the righteous view ;
See, ever-streaming tears their cheeks bedew ! 30
L 2 " Surely

11 " Surely (they cry) our glorious God is juft;
    " Will he not punifh fuch imperious duft ?
12 " If fuch profperity the wretch attends,
    " Whofe daring blafphemy high heav'n offends;
    " If wealth, if honours, to the impious flow,   35
    " Who fuch confummate infolence dare fhew;
13 " Vainly our hearts we've cleans'd from ev'ry ftain,
    " We've wafh'd our hands in innocence in vain.
14 " Why fuch continued anguifh do we bear ?
    " Why guard our actions with fuch fruitlefs care ?"   40
15 But foon thefe wild furmifes I reftrain'd ;
    Soon my complaining heart with awe I rein'd ;
    Left 'gainft my God I fhou'd have guilty been,
    And judg'd his conduct with the fons of men.
16 Yet anxious ftill, the latent caufe I fought ;   45
    Still the amazing fcene employ'd my thought ;
    Fruitlefs my fearch-----I no relief cou'd find ;
    A gloomy darknefs clouded ftill my mind.
17 When to thy temple, Lord, I bent my way ;
    There on my foul thou beam'd'ft a fudden day ;   50
    No more thy favours to the wicked wound ;
    Their fad, their fatal end I ftraitway found.
18 I faw on what a flipp'ry height they ftood,
    How vain the wealth that conftant to them flow'd ;
    What poor fupport 'twou'd prove, when o'er their head 55
    Thou fhou'dft the terrors of thy vengeance fpread.
19 How in a moment are they all deftroy'd !
    How are their honours and their riches void !
20 Like a mere fleeting dream at night they are ;
    Awhile they ftrike our fouls with doubt, with fear ;   60
    But when our God awakes, the terror's o'er,
    And they're defpis'd, who ftruck with dread before.
21 This 'fore I knew, what gloomy thoughts did roll
    Within my breaft ? what anguifh pain'd my foul ?
22 Stupid and dull, I like a brute became,   65
    Clouded with ignorance, and funk in fhame.
23 But now, fupported by thy pow'rful hand,
    Now that thy fecret will I underftand ;
24 Thro' thy propitious influence I revive,
    And in thy glory humbly hope to live.   70
25 Whom have I, gracious God, in heav'n but thee ?
    On earth, who mates thy love, thy clemency ?
26 Broke was my anguifh'd heart ; my fpirits fail'd,
    And a dead numbnefs o'er my frame prevail'd.

                                                    Thou

Thou with new vigour didſt my ſoul inſpire,   75
And gav'ſt my plaining heart her full deſire.
27 While on the wicked thy dread judgments fall,
And they, who thee deſpiſe, ſhall periſh all;
28 Thy will I'll follow-----thou, my only ſtay,
Oft to my ſoul thy goodneſs didſt diſplay;   80
Bleſt with thy love; from doubt, from danger free,
Continual anthems will I ſing to thee.

P S A L M *LXXIV.*

1 HOW long, O Lord, will thy dread anger hold?
   How long ſhall rav'ning wolves devour thy fold?
2 Remember, Lord, the purchaſe thou haſt made,
The tribes, redeem'd from bondage by thy aid,
The bleſt inheritance thou call'dſt thy own,   5
The hill of *Sion*, where thou'ſt fix'd thy throne.
3 Ariſe, juſt God, reſtrain the mad'ning foe,
That with ſuch impious pride and fury glow;
That, inſolent and blaſphemouſly vain,
Thy hallow'd temple with their hands profane.   10
4 Sounds the ſhrill trumpet, and the nations roar,
Not they who thee with humble hearts adore;
But thoſe thy foes, that vile rebellious race,
Who on thy ſacred tow'rs their ſtandards place.
5 Wild with ſucceſs, they range the city round,   15
They raze thy hallow'd temple to the ground;
The dread tremendous ruin, as it falls,
Hark! the dire cruſh! our ſinking hearts appalls.
So fall, when conquer'd by redoubled ſtrokes,
Down the ſteep mountain's ſide the tumbling oaks.   20
6 They all it's glorious ornaments deſtroy;
Beetles and bars their cruel hands employ;
7 View the whole fabrick, circled round with flame,
The fabrick ſacred to thy holy name.
8 Fully reſolv'd, they to each other ſay,   25
" Be this to *Salem*'s pride the final day;
" 'Bove other towns no longer let her ſoar;
" Fate threats her now, and ſhe ſhall rule no more."
9 Mean while, no ſigns of thy aſſiſtance; we,
No inſpir'd prophet, to conſole us, ſee;   30
Not one, who e'en a ſlender hope can give,
That thou thy wretched people wilt relieve.
10 How long, good God, ſhall our inſulting foes
Sport with thy people, and illude their woes;

How

How long wilt thou permit them to blafpheme,
With their reproachful taunts, thy facred name ? 35

11 Ah ! why from us thy mighty hand withdrawn ?
Ah ! why thy once-lov'd tribes left fo forlorn ?

12 Of old our leader thou, our guide haft been ;
For us thy wond'rous works all earth hath feen : 40

13 At thy command retir'd the foamy fea,
And with a double wall fecur'd our way ;
Then back at thy command obedient flows,
And with her furges overwhelms our foes.

14 The haughty tyrant, infolent and vain, 45
Fierce as the wildeft monfters of the main,
Sunk in her waves, and on the defart fhore
Was toft, for rav'nous vultures to devour :

15 Thou fpak'ft-----hard rocks a plenteous-ftream fupply ;
Thou fpak'ft------the rivers leave their channels dry. 50

16 Thine is the day, O God, and thine the night ;
The fun thou gildeft with his beamy light ;

17 Thou keep'ft the mad'ning fea within her bounds :
The earth thou ftrength'neft with her rocky mounds !
When rages winter with his horrid train, 55
Thou ftill with fuited warmth reviv'ft the plain ;
When fcorches fummer with it's fultry heat,
Thou fann'ft the air, and giv'ft a cool retreat.

18 And wilt not thou remember the difgrace,
Which caft the wicked on thy faithful race ? 60
Wilt thou forget the fhocking blafphemies,
Wherewith thy name tremendous they defpife ?

19 From their big infults free thy plaintive dove,
The once-bleft object of almighty love ;
Hear thy afflicted people, once thy boaft, 65
Nor in oblivion let their cries be loft :

20 O call that holy covenant to mind,
Which with moft folemn fanction thou didft bind :
For dreadful, dreary darknefs fhades our head,
And cruelty around, and rapine fpread. 70

21 O let not they, that love thy facred name,
The indigent, th' oppreft, return with fhame.

22 Arife, almighty Lord ; thy pow'r exert ;
Thine is the injur'd's caufe ; their caufe affert :
With rage befotted, lo ! the impious croud 75
Speak 'gainft thy pow'r their blafphemies aloud.

23 Forget not, Lord, their vile opprobious tongues,
Their big impieties, their ceafelefs wrongs ;

Still,

Still, ſtill their monſtrous villainies increaſe,
And with relentleſs hate they ſtill oppreſs. 80

P S A L M *LXXV.*

1 TO thee, O God, in ſongs of joy we'll raiſe
   The tuneful voice, and celebrate thy praiſe;
Thy great, thy wond'rous mercies we'll proclaim,
And ſing the glories of thy holy name.

2 " When comes th' appointed time to judge the earth, 5
  " I'll call (ſays God) my winged council forth,
  " And on that ſolemn, that tremendous day,
  " 'Fore them my righteous juſtice I'll diſplay.

3 " And at my preſence tho' this earth diſſolve,
  " Tho' dreadful fears her guilty ſons involve, 10
  " Yet firm I'll fix her in her wonted ſpace,
  " Strengthen her pillar, and confirm her baſe."

4 Ye ſenſeleſs fools, how oft have I in vain
Warn'd you, your wretched follies to refrain?
How oft, to leave the fatal road you trod, 15
Nor take up impious arms againſt your God?

5 Say, whence this ſtiff-neck'd, ſelf-will'd frenzy ſprings;
Whence this rebellion 'gainſt the king of kings?
On what frail feeble hopes have ye relied,
That thus you raiſe your creſts with haughty pride? 20

6 For not the raging *north*, nor roſy *eaſt*,
Nor yet the rainy *ſouth*, or ruddy *weſt*,
Can give you wealth, or fix you on a throne:

7 That ſov'reign pow'r pertains to God alone;
'Tis he that raiſes from the duſt the poor; 25
'Tis he brings down the haughty ſpirit low'r.

8 For lo! a flowing cup his hand divine
Extends, a cup that glows with purple wine;
Mix'd with a deadly poiſon is the draught;
'Fore him earth's trembling, guilty ſons are brought; 30
Lo! to the wicked is the potion ſet;
The wicked quaff-----perdition is their fate.

10 By me, all nations, and all ages, hear
The God of *Jacob* thus his will declare;

11 " Of impious men, that have my pow'r defied, 35
  " With fearful vengeance I'll confound the pride;
  " The humbly good, that in affliction ſigh,
  " I'll crown with bright rewards, and raiſe them high."

P S A L M *LXXVI.*

1 TO fancied gods while all the nations bend,
   Our faithful tribes th' almighty Lord attend;
   In *Judah* is his pow'r, his glory known;
2 *Salem's* his temple, *Sion* is his throne.
3 'Twas here he broke the sword, the shaft, the spear;   5
   And all the deadly implements of war.
4 What bright majestic terror round him shone,
   When he earth's mighty tyrants tumbled down?
5 Struck by his pow'r, they fell an easy prey;
   Sunk in eternal sleep their eyes, they lay.   10
6 Vain was the chariot, useless was the steed;
   Trembled at his rebuke their hearts with dread.
7 And just their fear, for who his wrath can stand?
   Who dare the thunder of his vengeful hand?
8 Did not, when he, in majesty array'd,   15
   Came down, propitious, to his servant's aid?
   Did not high heav'n the awful sentence hear?
   Was not th' astonish'd earth struck mute with fear?
10 His punishments, that on oppressors fall,
   Rejoice the good, the impious soul appall.   20
11 Ye tribes, that round his sacred temple dwell,
   Your victims offer, and his praises tell;
12 Vow to your God, who, dreadful in his wrath,
   Humbles the haughty monarchs of the earth.

P S A L M *LXXVII.*

1 TO thee, O Lord, I made my humble pray'r,
   Thee I implor'd, and gracious thou didst hear.
2 To thee alone in my distress I pray'd,
   With dreadful ills when I was sore dismay'd;
   To thee the live-long night held up my hands,   5
   Nor wou'd receive the solace of my friends.
3 On thee alone relying, thee I chose,
   To heal my heart, to dissipate my woes;
   My soul with deep, with bitter anguish pain'd,
   To thee I therefore heavily complain'd.   10
4 And well might I complain, for sleep no more
   Wou'd o'er my eyes exert his healing pow'r;
   Tho' on my limbs a heavy stupor hung,
   And my continued anguish chain'd my tongue.
5 'Twas then my mind revolv'd my former days,   15
   When thee I sung in sweet harmonious lays;

My

6 My grateful praifes on the tuneful lyre,
  The hymns of joy thy mercies did infpire;
  With thefe ideas long my foul was fraught,
  And thus wou'd I indulge the penfive thought: 20
7 " Ah! will th' all-high make me no more his care?
  " Shall I no more his gracious goodnefs fhare?
8 " Ah! will his mercy now no more prevail,
  " And is it poffible his truth fhould fail?
9 " Has he his great beneficence forgot?   25
  " Will dire refentment bring his love to nought?"
10 Soon I repented of the vain furmife;
  Thy ways of old I fet before my eyes,
  The ever-gracious deeds thy hand had done,
  The various mercies thou hadft conftant fhewn;   30
12 The griefs, the dangers, thou hadft chac'd away,
  The quick relief thou gav'ft without delay.
13 Yes; fov'reign ruler, I thy juftice fee;
  For truth, for mercy, who is like to thee?
14 To the whole earth the wonders of thy pow'r   35
  Shew'd thee the univerfal governor.
15 When ftruck proud *Pharaoh* with a dread alarm
  Thy favour'd tribes, them, by thy mighty arm,
16 Didft thou redeem; thy arm the waters faw,
  The troubled depths, and they beheld with awe.   40
17 The heavy clouds obey'd thy great command,
  And delug'd with their watery ftores the land;
18 Fell thy deftroying hail, thy thunders roar'd;
  Their rapid fires thy forky lightnings pour'd.
19 And when thy people *Pharaoh*'s fury fled;   45
  When *Mofes* and his facred brother led
  Them thro' the deep, and ftrait purfued the foe;
  Back on the hoftile bands the waters flow;
  Fain they'd retreat; but their attempts are vain;
  Sudden they perifh in th' o'er-whelming main: 50
  While, as his fleecy care the fhepherd leads,
  Thou guid'ft them thro' the fea; the fea recedes;
  Stood on a heap the fea at thy command;
  Secure they pafs, and joyful reach the ftrand.

P S A L M *LXXVIII.*

1 YE fons of *Ifrael*, faithful tribes, attend;
    A lift'ning ear to thefe my numbers lend;
2 My flowing numbers marvels fhall unfold,
  Which were in parables conceal'd of old;

M

Which

3 Which from our ancient fathers we have known ;   5
4 Which shall to late posterity be shewn :
  Yes; I, no simple bard, whom heav'n inspires
  (E'en now my soul celestial transport fires!)
  I will the wonders of th' Almighty sing,
  The pow'r, the praises, of our God, our king.   10
5 For, when he made with *Abr'ham's* favour'd line
  A league, confirm'd by sanctions most divine,
  Them his peculiar people when he chose,
  This, his determin'd will, he did impose,
  That they his law, the wonders he had done,   15
  For ever to their after-race make known ;
7 That, mindful of his mercies and his word,
  Firmly they might rely upon their Lord ;
  The statutes, that he had ordain'd, observe,
  And never from his dread commandments swerve :   20
8 Never, like their rebellious fathers, prove
  Ingrate and stubborn to almighty love ;
  Never, like them, distrust his gracious pow'r,
  But wait his mercy, and his name adore.
9 Ye sons of *Ephraim*, why, when strongly arm'd   25
  With bow, with spear, so dreadfully alarm'd ?
  Why fly your foes in the embattl'd field ?
  Why, when the fight began, so basely yield ?
10 Alas ! the sacred cov'nant they 'ad forgot,
  Their God's most holy law regarded not ;   30
11 Forgot the wonders of his mighty hand,
12 His glorious acts in *Egypt's* idol-land ;
  His glorious acts, that all their fathers saw,
  That struck proud *Pharaoh's*-harden'd heart with awe.
13 He for their passage made the sea divide ;   35
  Her waves a rampier form'd on either side ;
14 With a dun cloud he led them in the day ;
  By night a stream of fire directs their way ;
15 In the dry desart, fainting and athirst,
  They cried-----his ears their piteous plainings pierc'd.   40
  He from the rock his plenteous streams bestow'd,
  The rock he smote, and pour'd a limpid flood.
17 Yet still they sinn'd against his sov'reign pow'r,
  And by their faithless murmurs vex'd him sore :
18 Dar'd in their thankless hearts to tempt their God,   45
  And ask'd with highest insolence for food.
19 Great was their blasphemy, when thus they said ;
  " In the lone desart can he furnish bread ?

                                 " True;

20 " True; in our néed the veiny rock he fmote,
  " And in full torrents gufh'd the waters out. 50
  " Food to fupply, is fure beyond his pow'r,
  " And where of bread, of flefh, his fecret ftore?"
21 This heard the Lord, and ftrait his anger rofe;
  With dread refentment 'gainft his tribes he glows;
22 'Caufe they, tho' fuch great mercies they'd receiv'd, 55
  Still wanted faith, nor in his power believ'd.
23 Yet did he open ftrait the doors of heav'n;
24 Above their hopes, celeftial food was giv'n;
  In plenteous fhow'rs th' ambrofial manna fell,
  Meats, that did far all earthly cates excel. 60
25 O bleft refult of clemency divine!
  Meats, fuch as angels eat, he gave, benign;
26 He drove the *eaft wind* from the fields of air,
  And bad the *fouth* his flaggy wings prepare;
27 The *fouth* obey'd, and pour'd a feather'd flood, 65
  Birds of the richeft flavour for their food.
  O'er the aftonifh'd camp in heaps they lay,
  Thick as the fcatter'd fand along the fea.
29 And now they are with heavenly cates replete;
30 Yet ftill their lufts continue, while they eat, 70
31 E'en while they eat, the God, that's ever juft,
  Made them the victims of their wretched luft;
  In his dread fury on the camp he flew,
  And the moft valiant of their chieftains flew.
32 Yet vain th' inflictions of his vengeance prov'd; 75
  Nor yet his great beneficence remov'd
30 Their horrid guilt-----at length, provok'd, their God
  With all his rage and all his fury glow'd,
  Their vitals with a dread diftemper ftruck,
  Their wounded fouls with all his horrors fhook, 80
34 Driv'n, by his vengeance, him they own'd their Lord,
  His pow'r acknowledg'd, and his help implor'd;
35 Own'd, they fubfifted by his mighty aid,
  That he redeem'd them, and their foes difmay'd.
36 Yet this they only with their lips confeft; 85
  Conviction cou'd not reach their harden'd breaft;
37 Their vile demeanour, not their hearts, they chang'd,
  Their hearts from his bleft ftatutes ftill eftrang'd.
38 Still he in mercy wou'd their crimes forgive;
  Still in his favour he wou'd let them live; 90
  Full oft his fearful anger he forbore,
  And did to health, to peace, their fouls reftore;

39 For he confider'd them of mortal birth,
 That they were ftill but quicken'd lumps of earth ;
 Or empty fhadows of a fummer's day,
 That, like a fleeting wind, poft fwift away.   95

40 And yet how oft ungrateful did they prove
 To all the efforts of his tender love ;

41 Meafur'd almighty ftrength by their fhort line,
 And, obftinate, denied his pow'r divine !   100

42 Their great deliv'rance they remember'd not,
 Soon they the mercies of his arm forgot ;
 For them how he ftupendous wonders wrought,
 And 'gainft *Egyptian* rage their battles fought.

44 How with infected ftreams their rivers flow'd,   105
 Their limpid waters ting'd with filthy blood :

45 Range o'er their dwellings, the devouring fly,
 And marfhy frog, their palaces annoy ;

46 The locufts and deftructive beetles fwarm
 Around their fields, and do them dreadful harm :   110

47 Their vines are ruin'd by the beating hail,
 And o'er their trees the blafting frofts prevail :

48 His hail deftroys the cattle of the plain,
 And all their flocks are by his thunder flain :

49 Dread in his wrath, he all his vengeance pour'd,   115
 Full on their heads his indignation roar'd ;
 In heavieft trouble, in diftrefs they lay,
 And in-born furies on their vitals prey.

50 Stalks death around, in all his horrors clad,
 And beaft and man devouring plagues invade.   120

51 Hark ! what fad moans ! what unavailing cries !
 The favour'd fon, the father's darling, dies !
 Joy of his years, and heir to his domain !
 He dies ; and mourns parental love in vain !

52 Mean while, as leads the fwain his woolly care,
 Our God did for his tribes their way prepare ;   125

53 Fearlefs, they went ; and joyful reach the fhore,
 While the returning waves their foes devour.

54 Safely he brought them to the facred hill,
 That holy mount where chofe himfelf to dwell ;   130

55 For them the impious nations chac'd away,
 And made their fertile lands his people's prey.

56 Yet ftill provoking, they their God defied,
 Defpis'd his ftatutes, and his patience tried ;

57 Juft like their fathers they rebellious prov'd,   135
 And from the even path of duty rov'd ;

Like

Like a deceitful bow they turn'd, and foon
Their wonted blafphemy and crimes begun.

58 Their Lord eternal they no more obey'd,
But after gods, that were not gods, they ftray'd;　140
On each high hill their adorations pay
To images of brafs, of ftone, of clay.

59 This faw th' Almighty, and his anger rofe;
He now abhorr'd the people he had chofe;

60 Them of his glad'ning prefence he bereft,　145
And his own altar, his dear *Shiloh*, left:

61 His hallow'd ark no more in *Judah* ftands,
Whence beam'd his glorious light to diftant lands;
The facred monument of his people's peace,
Pledge of his awful law, the foes poffefs.　150

62 His people war with her fell train deftroys,
While with regardlefs ears he hears their cries.

63 Their lufty youth are by the flames devour'd;
Fall their hoar priefts by th' unrelenting fword;
No more the nuptial bed, the virgin-throng　155
Expect, or join the hymeneal fong;
No more the widows for their conforts figh,
And in the grave they unlamented lie.

65 At length his furious anger was appeas'd;
And foon the infults of the *heathen* ceas'd;　160
As from a heavy fleep our God arofe,
And pour'd his dreadful vengeance on our foes:

66 Struck with a quick alarm, they turn, they fly;
In vain-----for by his fatal fhafts they die;
And, while yon fun fhall fhine, continued fhame,　165
Continued infamy awaits their name.

67 Yet not to *Ephraim*, tho' his fons were brave,
Nor to *Manaffeh*, he the fceptre gave;

68 His favour'd choice the tribe of *Judah* prov'd;
The hill of *Sion* was the hill he lov'd.　170

69 There he his facred feat for ever plac'd,
His temple there with his bright prefence bleft;
Firm as the globe, the hallow'd dome fhall ftand,
Firm fhall remain, till nature's felf fhall end.

70 And him who tended long his fleecy care,　175

71 Who drove his fatlings to the paftures fair,
David, his fervant, has he call'd *his own*,
And fix'd the humble fhepherd on a throne;
O'er his own fav'rite people gives him fway,
And bids the fons of *Abraham* obey.　180

72 By him fupported, in his prowefs ftrong,
His flock with faithful care he 'as govern'd long ;
Protects them from the fury of the foe,
And teaches them the laws of heav'n to know.

P S A L M *LXXIX.*

1 THOU fov'reign Lord, that fill'ft our earth with dread,
  Shall impious foes thy heritage invade ?
Shall they thy facred, folemn dome-profane ?
Shall o'er thy favour'd tribes deftruction reign ?

2 Dead are the pious fouls that lov'd thy word,   5
Dead are they all, the victims of the fword :
They're to the wolves expos'd in open air ;
Lo ! their difmember'd limbs the vultures tear.

3 Round *Salem*'s walls flow fcarlet ftreams of blood,
As when the rains increafe th' impetuous flood ;   10
Their mangled carcaffes unburied lie,
And not one friend that will a grave fupply.

4 And both alike, the living and the dead,
A theme for laughter and contempt are made.

5 O gracious father, will thy dreadful ire   15
For ever rage, and fhall it burn like fire ?

6 Pour out thy fury rather on the race,
That not avow thy pow'r, thy law embrace :
Thofe impious kingdoms, blafphemoufly vain,
Who to invoke thy holy name difdain :   20

7 The ruin of thy people who refolve,
And in devouring flame their towns involve.

8 Recall not, Lord, our heinous crimes of yore,
And let thy wrath vindictive burn no more :
Quite overwhelm'd in killing woes we are ;   25
Prevent us with thy love ; in pity fpare.

9 Why fhou'd the *heathen* fpread their taunts abroad,
And blafphemoufly cry, " Where is their God ?"

10 To us extend thy clemency divine,
And let thy glory in our pardon fhine :   30
Affert thyfelf, O Lord, and 'fore our eyes
In all the terrors of thy vengeance rife ;
Revenge the blood of innocence they've fpilt,
And punifh, punifh their enormous guilt.

11 Thy pow'r exert, to heal the captive's grief,   35
To give him, from his galling chains, relief ;
Bid them in peace, in joy, in fafety, breathe,
Who're deftin'd by their cruel foes to death.

12 The vile reproach, the contumelies, that they
  Caſt on thy people, and on thee, repay; 40
  O let a ſev'n-fold puniſhment be theirs,
  In our deliv'rance while thy pow'r appears;
13 While we, great ſhepherd, thy peculiar flock,
  Make thee our whole ſupport, our ſtrength, our rock;
  And, in thy paſtures as we feed, diſplay 45
  Thy praiſe, thy pow'r, thy love, from day to day.

P S A L M LXXX.

1 O THOU (between the cherubims thy throne)
    Whom *Jacob*'s faithful race their ſhepherd own,
  Who feed'ſt thy *Iſraël* with a ſhepherd's care,
  Benign O liſt; attend our humble pray'r.
2 Thou to thy choſen tribes thy glory ſhew; 5
  Give them, the influence of thy pow'r to know;
  Their many woes thy inſtant help demand;
  O aid them, ſave them, by thy mighty hand.
3 Our heavy griefs to diſſipate is thine;
  The clouds diſperſe, when beams thy light divine. 10
4 Dread God of battles, will thy anger laſt?
  Prefer a fruitleſs pray'r thy tribes diſtreſt?
5 Their board with ever-ſtreaming tears bedew'd,
  Tears are their only drink, their only food.
6 We of our villain-foes are made the ſpoil, 15
  And, tho' they quarrel for their ſpoils the while,
  Yet ſtill with cruel, with inhuman pride,
  Our ſore diſtreſſes, ſcornful, they deride.
7 But all our griefs to heal, O Lord, is thine;
  The clouds diſperſe, when beams thy light divine. 20
8 A vine thou brought'ſt from *Pharaoh*'s hoſtile land;
  This vine thou planted'ſt with thy mighty hand;
9 To make it room, the nations drov'ſt away;
  Deep root ſhe took; and ſoon did ſhe diſplay
10 Her tendrils far, the mountains ſoon ſhe ſhades, 25
  And like the tow'ring, lofty cedar ſpreads,
11 Her fruitful boughs ſhe ſtretches to the ſea,
  To where *Euphrates* rolls his rapid way.
12 Ah! why does ſhe her broken fences mourn?
  Why left unto her foes a prey, a ſcorn? 30
13 Why lays the cruel boar her branches waſte?
  Why on her blooming fruits the beſtials feaſt?
14 Return, O God, and let thy mercy ſhine
  On this thy drooping, deſolated vine;

By

15 By thee 'twas planted, and by thee grew ſtrong ;　　35
　　By thee in all her pride ſhe flouriſh'd long ;
16 But now deſtroying flames her boughs devour ;
　　Laid level with the ground, ſhe blooms no more.
17 Indulgent father, kind aſſiſtance ſend ;
　　With thy almighty arm thy vine defend.　　40
　　O let the man, whom long thou didſt adorn
　　With pow'r, with honours, now no longer mourn ;
18 Reſtore us life, and we'll thy name adore,
　　And from thy ſacred ſtatutes turn no more.
19 All, all our griefs to heal, O Lord, is thine ;　　45
　　The clouds diſperſe, when beams thy light divine.

P S A L M *LXXXI.*

1　**I**N loftieſt ſtrains addreſs the mighty God ;
　　　To *Iſrael's* great redeemer chant aloud ;
2 Chant the glad pſalm, and to the timbrel join
　　The lute, the pſaltery, harmony divine !
3 Sound, ſound the clarion, and your joy diſplay ;　　5
　　Now is the ſtated feaſt, the ſolemn day ;
4 The ſacred ſolemn day, which heav'n ordain'd,
　　Which *Iſrael* ſwore t' obſerve, while time remain'd ;
5 The great memorial of *Egyptian* rage,
　　When nought cou'd *Pharaoh's* harden'd heart aſſuage ;　　10
　　When on the banks of *Nile,* ſad wand'rers, they
　　In direful bondage groan'd, and felt diſmay ;
　　When they a language heard, not underſtood ;
6 When bent their backs beneath the galling load.
7 " 'Twas then, in miſery ſunk, with griefs appall'd,　　15
　　" With fervent prayer (ſays God) on me you call'd ;
　　" On me you call'd, and I indulgent heard,
　　" Diſpers'd your woes, your road to freedom clear'd ;
　　" Enwrapt in clouds, I gave my ſacred law,
　　" In thunder ſpoke, and ſtruck your ſouls with awe ;　　20
　　" Your faith at *Meribah's* fam'd waters prov'd,
　　" Forgave your murmurs, and the cauſe remov'd.
8 " Hear, O my people, with attention hear,
　　" Hear, while my ſolemn promiſe I declare :
9 " If thou my laws, my ſtatutes, will obey,　　25
　　" And after other gods wilt ſcorn to ſtray :
　　" If to their altars thou'lt no victims bring,
10 " But only worſhip me, thy God, thy king,
　　" Thy God that from hard bondage ſet thee free,
　　" And pav'd thy way to peace, to liberty ;　　30
　　　　　　　　　　　　　　　　　　　　" On

" On thee I'll bleſſings 'bove thy hopes beſtow,
" And ev'ry ſolid good to thee ſhall flow ;
11 " Vainly I ſaid ; my people wou'd not hear,
" But to my promiſe turn'd a liſtleſs ear :
12 " Therefore I left them to their worſt of foes,   35
" Their ſenſeleſs ſelves, the guides themſelves had choſe ;
" Therefore I left them, madly to fulfil
" The wretched dictates of their headſtrong will.
13 " But Oh ! that they had heard me, and obey'd,
" Nor ever from the way I taught them ſtray'd !   40
14 " Me their ſupport, with glory they had reign'd,
" And o'er their foes a noble conqueſt gain'd.
15 " I had not then maintain'd the odious cauſe
" Of thoſe that hate me, and deſpiſe my laws ;
" To *Iſrael* they had yielded ; *Iſrael*'s God   45
" Eternal rule on *Iſrael* had beſtow'd :
16 " Them with what happy affluence I had bleſt !
" The fields had furniſh'd a continual feaſt ;
" From the hard rock had guſh'd ambroſial rills,
" Sweet as the *nectar*, which the bee diſtils.   50

P S A L M. LXXXII.

1   IN vain perverſely, princes, you ſurmiſe,
     God views your judgments with regardleſs eyes ;
Lo ! in the midſt he ſtands, your ways beholds,
And thus in thunder his dread wrath unfolds.
2 " How long thus partial will ye judge ? how long   5
" Support their cauſe, who in their guilt are ſtrong ?
3 " Ah ! rather the diſtreſſed orphan view,
" And to the cauſe of innocence be true ;
4 " Ah ! free the wretched from th' oppreſſive foe,
" And do the poor the juſtice that you owe.   10
5 " Vainly I warn them ; obſtinately blind ;
" A fatal error chains their ſtubborn mind ;
" In guilt they're reſolute, and won't obſerve
" The dire reſult, when they from juſtice ſwerve.
6 " I call'd you gods, to you the pow'r I gave,   15
" To ſlay th' oppreſſor, and th' oppreſt to ſave ;
" On you my own prerogative beſtow'd,
" To curb the villain, and protect the good.
7 " But now grim death, with all his horrid train,
" Shall ſoon convince you, that you are but men,   20
" Shall ſink your boaſted honours in the grave,
" And make you equal with the meaneſt ſlave.

N   Yes ;

8 Yes; Lord *Jehovah*, thou vindictive rife;
  To thee afcend the orphan's plaintive cries,
  Judge thou the earth, and make fell tyrants know   25
  Thou rul'ft, impartial, all the realms below.

P. S A L M · *LXXXIII.*

1 NO more be ftill, juft God; no more delay;
    Speak in their caufe, who thy commands obey;
2 For lo! with lofty crefts exult thy foes,
  With loud tumultuous roar they've all arofe:
3 Fix'd are their counfels; all their fchemes they bend ·   5
  'Gainft thofe whom thou haft promis'd to defend.
4 " Hafte (they cry all) be this our fole employ,
  " Thefe favour'd tribes, this *Ifrael* to deftroy."
5 See, with what firm envenom'd hate they join,
  And 'gainft thy people and thy law combine.   10
6 *Idume, Moab, Amalek,* confpire,
  With *Gebal, Ammon, Ifhmael*'s race and *Tyre;*
  Nor has *Philiftia* her defeats forgot,
  And proud *Affyria* joins the fons of *Lot.*
9 But let them fall by our avenging hands,   15
  As perifh'd *Sifera* and his hoftile bands:
  At *Kifhon* perifh'd they, and with their blood
  Ting'd, as it gently ftream'd, his ancient flood:
  Their carcaffes along his margin lay,
  To rav'ning vultures and fell wolves a prey.   20
11 As *Oreb* fled and mighty *Zeb* in vain,
  As *Zeba* and *Zalmunna* bit the plain;
  Who fiercely faid; " Be ours their wide domains,
  Their fenced cities, and their hallow'd fanes;"
  So let their nobles and their princes fall;   25
  So in thy direful wrath confume them all;
13 Swift let them fly, while follow we behind,
  And drive them far like ftubble 'fore the wind.
14 As crackling fires along the mountains roar,
  And the tall honours of the grove devour,   30
15 'Gainft them fend forth the tempeft of thy wrath,
  And let thy whirlwinds fink them all in death.
16 Their faces cover with reproach, with fhame,
  That e'en their woes thy Godhead may proclaim;
17 With terror, with affright, their fouls confound;   35
  A dread example to the nations round;
18 That all may know, *Jehovah* is the Lord,
  And that his name may be by all ador'd.

P S A L M *LXXXIV*.

1 HOW glorious, Lord, thy temple? what desires
   Fill my whole soul, O God? what rapture fires?
How asks my glowing heart the glad employ?
My limbs, my very bones, demand the joy.
3 Nigh thee, secure, her nest the sparrow builds;   5
Thy sacred altar to the swallow yields
Fit refuge for her young; in artless lays
Their sweet melodious throats pour forth thy praise,
4 Thrice happy all who in thy temple dwell!
Thy pow'r, thy praises, they shall constant tell,   10
5 Thrice happy they, who on their God rely,
And with their victims to his altar hie!
6 Thro' the dry vale as they direct their way,
Their thirst the cooling riv'let shall allay;
To fill their cisterns, falls the kindly rain,   15
While the vow'd victims to their God are slain.
8 Dread God of battles, hear thy servant's pray'r;
O to his pious vows incline thy ear;
9 'Tis thy *anointed* pleads; his shield art thou;
Thy own *anointed* with indulgence view.   20
10 One day within thy courts to him appears,
A lot more glorious than a thousand years:
The meanest office there I'd nobler own,
Than 'mid the wicked an exalted throne.
11 For, like the beamy monarch of the day,   25
Dost thou the glories of thy light display;
Thou, like a shield, thy servants dost defend,
And all the blessings of thy mercy send;
No blessing to the righteous thou'lt deny;
12 -----Thrice happy they, that will on thee rely!   30

P S A L M *LXXXV.*

1 THO' oft, O Lord, we've felt thy heavy wrath,
   And oft thy vengeance menaces with death,
Yet still thy people have thy mercy known,
Still hath thy great beneficence been shewn:
2 Our heinous crimes against thee thou'st forgot,   5
And in oblivion hid our ev'ry fault;
3 Benign hast heard us, when we did implore,
And bad thy dreadful fury rage no more.
4 Now then, indulgent God, propitious turn,
Nor 'gainst thy people let thine anger burn;   10

5 Muſt we thy dread reſentment ever bear ?
  And ſhall our after-race thy vengeance ſhare ?
6 Will now no more thy goodneſs bid us live,
  And in eternal anguiſh muſt we grieve ?
7 Once more, ah ! let forgiving mercy reign,   15
  Save us, O Lord, nor let us plead in vain.
8 Long have I waited for thy pow'rful word,
  That to our ſouls will peace, will bliſs, afford ;
  Long have I waited for the gracious ſign
  Of pard'ning love, of clemency divine ;   20
  That, if thy people wou'd no more offend,
  Soon thou wou'dſt ſolace and aſſiſtance ſend.
9 And ſure to them thy great ſalvation's near,
  Who love thy holy law, thy name who fear.
10 Yes ; joyful ſoon ſhall truth and mercy meet, 25
  Juſtice and pleaſing peace in tranſport greet :
11 Down from above the heav'n-born maids deſcend ;
  See, golden plenty on their ſteps attend ;
12 Bleſt with their happy influence, teeming earth
  Shall give to all her blooming produce birth ; 30
  Her corn, her wine, her oil, ſhall joyous yield,
  And cloath with verdure the rejoicing field.
13 Where'er our gracious Lord directs his way,
  There truth, there love, there juſtice, hold the ſway ;
  Thence fly oppreſſion, wrong, deceit and fraud, 35
  Thence quick they fly, by his dread preſence aw'd.

P S A L M *LXXXVI.*

1 TO thee, good God, in my diſtreſs I plead,
    Benign O hear me ; haſten to my aid ;
2 To my too juſt complaints propitious be,
  And ſave the pious ſoul that truſts in thee.
3 From morn to even heavily I ſigh,   5
  And ſhall I vainly on my God rely ?
4 On thee my ſoul depends in her diſtreſs ;
  O yet with thy enliv'ning preſence bleſs.
5 For good art thou, and ready to forgive ;
  Who call on thee ſincere, in thee ſhall live. 10
6 O hear attentive, while to thee I ſue ;
  My ſuffering innocence with pity view ;
7 Thee in my deep affliction I invoke ;
  For thee in trying times I've prov'd my rock.
8 Not one among the fancied gods like thee ; 15
  Not one can mate thy pow'r, thy majeſty.

9 The nations all fhall glorify thy name,
And hail almighty pòw'r with loud acclaim ;
10 For great árt thou ; the wonders thou haft done
Declare to all, that thou art God alone. 20
11 Teach me to thy bleft dome, th' unerring road ;
Compofe my foul, that fhe may praife her God.
12 Thee fhall fhe praife, and thee fhall fhe adore,
Thy name, thy pow'r, extol, till time's no more.
13 To her from thee continual bleffings flow ; 25
And oft thou'ft fav'd her from the depths below.
14 When men of violence againft me rofe,
When all the villain-rout commenc'd my foes ;
When with invet'rate hate my life they fought,
And fet thy dread omnipotence at nought : 30
15 'Twas then, compaffionate, thou didft relieve,
Didft to my anguifh'd heart fweet folace give.
16 O ftill, while now my cruel foes invade,
Thy fervant ftrengthen with thy mighty aid ;
17 That they with wonder and with fhame may fee, 35
I ftill have got a pow'rful friend in thee ;
That from thy clemency, fuccefs I have ;
That thou thy chofen fhepherd ftill wilt fave.

P S A L M *LXXXVII.*

1 'BOVE all our cities does bright *Sion* prove
The deareft object of almighty love ;
Sion, high feated on a lofty hill,
Where bleft *Jehovah* takes delight to dwell.
3 O Queen of nations ! O exalted theme ! 5
What tongue can juftly celebrate thy fame ?
4 Will *Babylon* to mate thy fplendor dare ?
With thee will *Rahab*'s haughty town compare ?
Soon fhall their vain, their empty boafts be fhewn ;
They foon fhall thy fuperior glories own ; 10
Nor, proud *Philiftia*, thou, nor lofty *Tyre*,
Nor *Ethiopia*'s towns to fame afpire ;
5 With *Sion*'s city ye conteft in vain ;
Long 'bove you all triumphant fhe fhall reign ;
By God himfelf are her foundations laid, 15
And he'll uphold her with his mighty aid.
6 Who o'er th' extended world will not aver,
Who will not boaft, that he belongs to her ?
7 Thy wond'rous beauties fhall attune the lyre ;
Thy glories fhall the raptur'd voice infpire ; 20

If

If aught befitting thee can fill my tongue,
Thee will I make my conftant, only fong;
If e'er my foul conceives a lofty lay,
Thy fame, dear city, fhall my verfe difplay.

P S A L M *LXXXVIII.*

1 O THOU, on whofe bleft mercy I rely,
　　Humbly to thee, by day, by night, I cry;
2 Turn not, indulgent God, thy face away,
　But gracious hear, when in diftrefs I pray;
3 Immers'd my anguifh'd foul in dreadful woe,　　　5
　E'en now fhe's finking to the depths below;
4 Languid my limbs, my ftrength, my vigour fled,
　Soon, foon fhall I be number'd with the dead;
5 Like his pale carcafe mould'ring in the grave,
　Whofe life thy fov'reign juftice wou'd not fave;　　10
　In youth's full bloom who by the jav'lin dies,
　Clos'd in a dread eternal fleep his eyes;
6 In death's low dungeon thus confin'd, fhall I,
　Wrapt in amazing, difmal darknefs, lie.
7 Still thy afflictive hand does prefs me fore,　　　15
　And all thy threat'ning ftorms around me roar:
8 Far from my prefence fly my wonted friends;
　Me in my fad diftrefs not one attends;
　Shock'd at my wretched fate, they hafte away,
　And leave me to my killing griefs a prey.　　　20
9 Mean while, mine eyes, my hands, I lift to thee,
　And in deep anguifh plead thy clemency.
10 Wilt thou thy wonders to the dead difplay,
　Or can the dead their adoration pay?
11 Shall the drear tomb thy glorious mercy fhew?　　25
　The gloomy grave thy gracious goodnefs know?
12 Shall dreadful filence celebrate thy pow'r?
　Shall everlafting night thy truth adore?
13 Conftant to thee I've cried, all-clement Lord,
　Conftant thy faving mercy I've implor'd.　　　30
14 Ah! why doft thou thy pow'rful aid forbear?
　Ah! why regardlefs hear my urgent pray'r?
15 E'en from my tender years I've known my grief,
　Nor from thy terrors have I found relief;
16 Thy terrors that diftract my heart with fear,　　35
　Thy terrors that reduce me to defpair;
17 Thy dreadful terrors that my foul furround,
　Like rain that deluges the fertile ground.

Helplefs

18 Helpleſs I lie, deſerted by my friends ;
No kind companion his aſſiſtance lends ;   40
L f in my ſorrows to myſelf alone,
Heaves my griev'd heart, and piteouſly I moan.

P S A L M LXXXIX.

1 THE glorious ſubject of my tuneful ſong
    Be thou, O God------to thee my ſtrains belong.
While laſts the ſun, while times to times ſucceed,
Thy goodneſs in my numbers ſhall be read.

2 For ſure the orbs in yon etherial plain   5
To their primœval *nought* return again,
Ere thou the wonders of thy mercy ceaſe,
Or 'gainſt thy ſacred covenant tranſgreſs.

3 Thy ſacred covenant with *David* made,
4 That, while yon lights the fields of air pervade,   10
While ſtands this ſolid earth upon her baſe,
While knows old *ocean* his appointed ſpace,
His progeny ſhall ſit upon the throne,
And *Iſrael*'s faithful tribes their rule ſhall own.

5 Thee, great *Jehovah*, thee the heav'nly hoſt   15
Adore, and make thy mighty works their boaſt ;
Thy truth the righteous make their conſtant theme,
Sing all thy mercies, and extol thy name.

6 With thee compar'd, O Lord, how meanly ſhew
The thrones above, the ſceptred kings below ?   20
7 Th' etherial myriads tremble at thy nod ;
Fear earth's imperious lords th' Almighty God.
8 Dread God of battles, who is like to thee ?
Who mates thy pow'r, thy truth, thy majeſty ?
9 Thou rein'ſt the fury of the ſwelling main,   25
And doſt the madneſs of her waves reſtrain ;
10 Th' *Egyptian* tyrant felt thy vengeful hand ;
Feel all, who dare thy ſov'reign rule withſtand :
Thine are the bright celeſtial worlds above
Thine is the earth------by thy command they move ;   30
Earth's varied bleſſings to thy love we owe ;
From thee, Creator-Lord, from thee they flow.
12 Thee the rude *north*, and rainy *ſouth*, obey,
And where the ſun begins, where ends the day,
Bleſt *Tabor* ſeated in the glowing *weſt*,   35
Bright *Hermon*, gladden'd by the beamy *eaſt*.
13 Strong is thy arm, reſiſtleſs is thy hand ;
14 Nigh to thy throne bright truth, ſtern juſtice, ſtand ;

Full

Full in thy view sweet clemency appears,
Bleft attribute! that calms our pious fears.

15 Thrice happy they, that hear thy gracious call,   40
Flock to thy fane, and 'fore thy altar fall!
On them with kindlieft ray thy light shall shine;

16 Daily they feel the joys of love divine;
Rais'd by thy goodnefs to the higheft blifs,   45

17 Pow'r, empire, glory, shall they long pofsefs;

18 Their ftrong fupport, their mighty leader thou,
They gain a glorious conqueft o'er the foe.

19 His facred prophet hear, ye fons of men;
By him th' Almighty fpeaks, nor fpeaks in vain: 50
" *David*, my fervant, from his low eftate,
" I've rais'd, and plac'd him on the royal feat;
" With kingly majefty I've him array'd,
" And fprinkled with my facred oils his head.

21 " To him I'll ftrength and nervous force impart,   55
" And with firm courage fortify his heart;

22 " Brave, he shall fcorn the foe's proud menaces,
" Nor villain-fchemes shall have 'gainft him fuccefs:

24 " True to my word, affiftance I'll fupply,
" And 'bove the clouds will raife his glory high.   60

25 " E'en from the fea the nations he shall fway,
" To where *Euphrates* rolls his rapid way:

26 " Me his fupport, his father he shall call,
" To me, as to his God, shall proftrate fall:

27 " Him with peculiar honour I will grace,   65
" As loves the fire the firft-born of his race;
" 'Bove other potentates I'll raife his name,
" And fet him foremoft in the lifts of fame.

28 " Nor to the prefent is my love confin'd,
" Nor to himfelf alone the fanctions bind;   70

29 " I'll to his progeny the throne fecure,
" And, long as beams the fun, shall laft their pow'r;

30 " But, if his children from my ftatutes ftray,

31 " Spurn at my laws, and not my will obey,

32 " Soon for the vile tranfgreffion they shall fmart;   75
" And foon I'll punish their rebellious heart.

33 " Yet shan't my mercy my own *David* leave;
" My covenant I made not, to deceive;

34 " Faithful and firm, I'll to my word remain;
" What once I've faid, shall man oppofe in vain.   80

35 " And by my holy felf to him I fwore,
" (And ne'er shall he my broken oath deplore):

" Till

36 " Till dies the world, till time no more runs on,
  " His bleft pofterity fhall fill the throne ;
37 " To this be witnefs, all ye lights above ;   85
  " When fails his race, no more your *orbits* move."
38 Thy gracious promife this-----but now, alas !
  From thy anointed thou haft hid thy face ;
39 Thy covenant forgot, and now caft down,
  For hoftile feet to trample on, his crown.   90
40 His cities thou'ft laid open to the foe ;
  Their walls difmantled, and their tow'rs brought low.
41 We're fall'n a prey to all the nations round ;
  With their infulting taunts our fouls they wound ;
42 Supported by thy hand, victorious they   95
  Highly exult, and with fuccefs are gay.
43 Edgelefs our fwords, we vainly dare the field,
  Are foon defeated, and with fhame we yield ;
44 Our pride, our glory, in the duft are laid,
  And dreadful dreary darknefs fhades our head :   100
45 In vile difhonour, in diftrefs we lie,
  Few are our days, and immature we die.
46 How long, O Lord, will laft thy dreadful ire ?
  Shall burn thy fury like confuming fire ?
47 Remember, Lord, how fhort the life of man ;   105
  Surely thou'ft not created us in vain !
48 But a few days we breathe the vital air,
  And thofe few days are clouded all with care,
  From death's dire call not one his foul can fave,
  And foon we're mould'ring in the gloomy grave.   110
49 Where are thy wonted tender mercies flown ;
  When firft thou fet'ft thy *David* on a throne ?
50 O view the killing fcorn, the fore diftrefs,
  Wherewith our impious foes thy tribes diftrefs ;
  Their fhocking infults in my breaft I bear,   115
  While they their horrid blafphemies declare ;
51 With infolent derifion while they fay,
  " He'll come----your promis'd king-----await the day-----
  " Your *Chrift* will come (they cry) the prince of peace,
  " And then, belike, your miferies will ceafe !"   120
52 But let them fneer-----to their confufion, they
  Shall feel his terrors at th' appointed day ;
  Our *Chrift* will come-----thy judgments he'll proclaim,
  And all the earth fhall tremble at thy name.

O   P S A L M

P S A L M *XC.*

1   ALMIGHTY Lord, e'er fince the world began,
          Great hath been thy beneficence to man ;
     E'er fince this earth firft run her annual round,
     In thee her thanklefs fons defence have found.
2   Still thou'rt the fame, and ever waft the fame,   5
     Ere yet the world affum'd this beauteous frame,
     Ere yet the high, the lofty hills appear'd ;
     Ere yet the glad'ning day gay mortals chear'd ;
     Ere fpread dun night her horrors all abroad,
     Thou art the fame, the everlafting God.   10
3   But thou haft giv'n fhort fpace to man on earth ;
     Soon fleet the winged minutes from his birth
     To that dark hour, when all his fchemes are vain,
     And to his parent-duft he goes again.
4   'Fore thee glide fwift a thoufand years away ;   15
     To thee they feem a fleeting winter's day ;
     Sudden they pafs, and ftrait no more are feen,
     And leave no trace, to tell us, they have been.
5   They roll impetuous like a rapid ftream ;
     Infenfibly they leave us like a dream ;   20
     Well to the grafs we may our lives compare ;
6   The grafs that looks at morn fo frefh, fo fair,
     That with it's verdant fpires enchants the fight,
     But hangs the head, and withers ere 'tis night.
7   Yet not with life's fhort period we're diftreft,   25
     As when thy dreadful anger ftrikes the breaft ;
8   For whate'er errors in our bofoms roll,
     Whate'er bafe paffions hold in chains the foul,
     Howe'er conceal'd, or kept from open day,
     Does thy all-feeing eye, O God, furvey ;   30
9   And while thy vengeance ftrikes us with defpair,
     Swifter than thought, life vanifhes to air.
10   For fev'nty years while goes his rounds the fun,
     To man 'tis giv'n his ftated courfe to run ;
     Haply his ftrength holds out ten winters more ;   35
     But then all folid joys of life are o'er ;
     On feeble age unnumber'd cares attend,
     Unnumber'd griefs that but with life fhall end ;
11   And, if our God ftrict juftice fhou'd demand,
     Ah ! who can bear his dread avenging hand ?   40
12   Teach us our fhort-liv'd period to difcern,
     That we the road to heav'n, to blifs, may learn ;

                                              Benign

13 Benign O hear us, and thine anger ceafe;
   Return, O Lord, and calm our fouls to peace.
14 O let thy mercy fill our hearts with joy,   45
   That our remaining hours we may employ
15 In peaceful fcenes, devoid of griefs, of fears,
   Free from the mis'ries of our former years.
16 Thy glorious works, the wonders of thy pow'r,
   Shew to thy fervants, that they may adore;   50
   And, that their off-fpring may thy laws obey,
   Thy great, thy awful attributes, difplay.
17 And let, O God, thy clemency divine
   With happy influence on thy chofen fhine,
   That ev'ry action of our life may prove,   55
   Thy grace directs us, profpers us thy love.

P S A L M *XCI.*

1 TO heav'n who trufts his fortunes and his life,
     Tho' rage around contention, broil and ftrife;
Tho' wild uproar and dire confufion fway,
His God will be his firm fupport and ftay.
2 Thou then bad fate and her affaults defy;   5
Thou to thy God for fafe protection fly;
Call him thy refuge, on his pow'r depend,
And he will ever, ever be thy friend.
3 From dark defigns of crafty men he'll free,
From all their toils will give thee liberty;   10
In fatal times, when rage difeafes round,
Thy great preferver he will ftill be found.
4 O'er thee his fhelt'ring wings fhall he expand;
Firm, firm beneath almighty care thou'lt ftand;
Nor ever to thy adverfe fortunes yield,   15
The God of battles, thy defence and fhield.
5 Secure he'll guide thee in the gloomy night,
From dangers fafe, as in the mid-day-light;
Secure he'll lead thee in the open day,
Nor foes, nor wars, nor terrors, fhall difmay.   20
7 In battle tho' ten thoufand round thee fall,
Thy guarded heart no perils fhall appall.
8 Mean while with joy the wicked thou fhalt view
Sink in the mis'ries that their crimes purfue.
9 For heav'n's high God thy refuge thou haft made,   25
And on his mercy haft relied for aid;
10 Therefore thy dwelling hears no big alarm;
No fad mifchance thy peaceful foul fhall harm:

11 And to his angels he has giv'n command,
 To watch thy fteps, to guide thee by the hand ;　　30
 O'er wilds, o'er cliffs, o'er defarts, thee to lead,
 That, free from bruifes, thou fecure may'ft tread :
13 That thou not fear, whene'er thou pafs the brake,
 The crefted bafilifk or fcaly fnake ;
 That thou undaunted may'ft the tiger meet,　　35
 And crufh the lordly lion with thy feet.
14 For fays th' almighty Lord, " 'Caufe me he loves,
 " My name adores, and my dread law approves,
 " His foul I'll guard, and foon exalt him high ;
15 " To me, his God, he in diftrefs fhall cry ;　　40
 " Him ftrait I'll hear, from all his terrors free,
 " And raife him to imperial dignity ;
16 " A length of days upon him fhall attend,
 " And joys immortal, joys that ne'er fhall end."

P S A L M *XCII.*

1 WHAT nobler fubject can the foul employ,
　　When feels the pious heart fublimer joy,
 Than when the praifes of her God fhe fings,
 And chants the glories of the king of kings ?
2 At night his truth, his honour to difplay,　　5
 His clemency, his mercies in the day ?
3 Whether the lofty theme the voice infpire,
 Whether it tunes the pfaltery and the lyre.
4 When my wrapt foul thy wonders meditate,
 What namelefs tranfports o'er my heart dilate ?　　10
5 Thy glorious wonders ! far beyond the ken
 Of earth's untoward fons, of impious men ;
7 Of men, the fhort-liv'd fhadows of a day,
 Who, like the blooming grafs, awhile look gay ;
 And, like the grafs, that fades, that withers foon,　　15
 Lofe quick their ftrength, their beauty, and are gone.
8 While permanent thy glory, Lord moft high,
 To endlefs time fhines forth thy majefty.
9 What dreadful fate attends thy ftubborn foes ?
 What fearful perils ! O what countlefs woes !　　20
10 Difpers'd, they fall ; while health, while vigour's mine,
 And thy bleft ointments on my temples fhine :
11 While my glad eyes with ceafelefs tranfport view
 Inevitable death their fteps purfue ;
 While, to my foul's defire, their fate fhe hears------　　25
 The welcome tidings fill my ravifh'd ears.

As

12 As high in *Lebanon* the cedar grows,
   As spreads th' aspiring palm her lofty boughs,
13 The righteous flourish long-----deep-rooted, they,
   Within thy courts, look ever green and gay ;   30
14 Loaded with fruits, yet constantly in bloom,
   No frosts shall nip them, and no blasts consume.
15 This solemn truth that all the earth may know,
   Our God is never to the good a foe ;
   Injustice hates, and equity approves,   35
   And humble innocence protects and loves.

P S A L M *XCIII.*

1 THE mighty Lord, the great *Jehovah* reigns ;
   Who form'd the worlds, and still the worlds sustains ;
   The Lord, who gives to humble worth his aid,
   Girded with strength, in majesty array'd.
2 Firm and unmoveable his awful throne,   5
   His pow'r no *flux*, no change of time has known.
3 Let the wild stormy sea tumultuous roar,
   And threaten with her turbid waves the shore ;
   He stays her mad'ning fury at his will ;
   Aw'd by his dread behest, her waves are still.   10
5 What once our God ordains, is firm and sure ;
   What he once bids, for ever shall endure ;
   Long as this solid world shall stand, O Lord,
   Shall last the solemn dictates of thy word.

P S A L M *XCIV.*

1 COME forth, O thou, whose dread avenging arm
   Strikes impious guilt with horror and alarm ;
2 Come forth, proclaim thy judgments all aloud,
   Thy dire inflictions on the haughty proud.
3 How long shall they, who have thy laws abhorr'd,   5
   Boast in their shocking crimes ?-----how long, O Lord ?
4 Elated with their guilt, how long look high,
   And 'gainst thine honour vent their blasphemy ?
5 With dreadful woes thy people they oppress,
   They load them with the most severe distress.   10
6 They the 'lorn widow and the orphan slay,
   They wait t' ensnare the trav'ller in his way ;
7 And yet they boast, their crimes thou wilt not see,
   That *right* and *wrong* are all the same to thee.

At

8 At length, ye liftlefs wretches, ope your eyes,   15
   Ere 'tis too late, learn knowledge, and be wife.
9 Blind does the God, that form'd the eye, appear,
   And deaf the fov'reign Lord that fram'd the ear ?
10 Who leads his fervants in the perfect way,
   Shall he not punifh them that difobey ?   20
11 Alas ! he knows the inmoft thoughts of men,
   Vain all your hopes, and all your counfels vain.
12 Thrice happy they, who feel the chaft'ning God,
   Who learn from him, of life, of blifs, the road !
13 In adverfe times their fainting fouls he'll fave ;   25
   While drop the wicked in the gaping grave.
14 For he'll not caft his heritage away,
   Nor leave them to their foes a guardlefs prey ;
15 He'll fix ftern juftice on her awful feat,
   And all his fervants to her throne direct.   30
16 With me againft the wicked who will rife ?
   Who 'gainft oppreffion kind relief fupplies ?
17 In the drear tomb I'd long agone been laid,
   Had not th' Almighty haften'd to my aid.
18 Vainly againft the danger I had ftrove,   35
   If not fupported by his pow'rful love.
19 'Twas he gave folace in my deep diftrefs,
   And calm'd the cares that did my foul deprefs.
20 " Will heav'n (I faid) with vile oppreffors join,
   " Who 'gainft the guiltlefs craftily combine ;   40
   " Their crimes who cover with a fair pretence,
   " And aim to fbed the blood of innocence ?"
22 But me, O fov'reign ruler, thou'lt defend,
   My rock thou art, thy pow'rful aid thou'lt fend ;
23 By their own arts the wicked thou'lt confume,   45
   Their own bafe fchemes fhall bring them to the tomb.

P S A L M *XCV.*

1 **A**PPROACH, ye tribes ; with one according voice
   Sing to your God, and in his name rejoice ;
2 Your faviour he ; let gratitude infpire
   The fong harmonious ; join with it the lyre.
3 He's Lord fupreme, the world's dread governor,   5
   Nor mate with him the other gods in pow'r.
4 His hand fupports our earth upon her bafe ;
   From him the cloud-topp'd mountains hold their place ;
5 Within his depths old ocean he reftrains,
   And his dread hand form'd hills and lawns and plains.   10

With

6 With bended knee 'fore your creator fall,
  With hands uplifted on *Jehovah* call ;
7 He is our God ; we in his paftures rove,
  And long fhall we enjoy almighty love,
8 If we the dictates of his law obey,   15
  Nor from his facred ftatutes wilful ftray :
  Stray, like our fathers in the days of yore,
  When they *Arabia*'s defarts wander'd o'er,
  When, tho' by conftant miracles he prov'd
  His boundlefs pow'r, ftill were their hearts unmov'd ;   20
  Still by their murmurs they provok'd his wrath,
  And tempted him to punifh them with death.
10 For forty years he their impatience bore ;
  At length his mercy wou'd forgive no more ;
  " Diftracted fure (he faid) thefe people are ;   25
  " Their God they know not-----by myfelf I fwear,
  " That they the promis'd land fhall ne'er enjoy,
  " But in thefe wild and defart plains fhall die."

P S A L M XCVI.

1 IN loftieft ftrains our fov'reign Lord adore,
  In ftrains, ye fons of men, untun'd before ;
2 Sing, fing his name ; with praife approach his throne,
  And let his pow'r in joyous hymns be fhewn :
3 His glory to the nations round declare,   5
  His mighty works let all the people hear :
4 Great is our God, and highly to be prais'd,
  Far 'bove the gods that human pride hath rais'd ;
5 Gods that to human madnefs ow'd their birth ;
6 While form'd *Jehovah* heav'ns and feas and earth.   10
  'Fore him authority and pow'r appear ;
  Beauty and ftrength in his bright prefence are.
7 Ye nations all that by his goodnefs live,
  The honour due unto the Godhead give ;
8 Grateful, his great unfathom'd glory fing,   15
  And to his facred courts your victims bring.
9 In feftal pomp his hallow'd dome draw near,
  And hail his name with reverential fear.
10 Say to the *heathen*, that our Lord is God,
  That worlds are govern'd by his awful nod ;   20
  To him that earth her firm foundation owes,
  And that he rules by equitable laws.
11 Rejoice, ye heav'ns-----thou earth, exult with joy-----
  Thou air, thou fea-----be this the glad employ

Of

Of all that breathe in earth, in fea, in air   25
12 Their joyous tranfports let the fields declare,
    Smile, fmile, ye woods ; let flow'rs, let fruits around
    Adorn your boughs ; let verdure cloath the ground ;
13 Be gay, all nature, for he comes, he comes ;
    The judge, th' impartial judge, he now affumes ;   30
    He comes the righteous from their foes to free,
    He comes to rule the world with equity.

P S A L M   *XCVII.*

1   **O**U R fov'reign Lord has univerfal fway ;
      Let earth, let all her ifles, their joy difplay ;
2 All, all their great almighty ruler own,
    On truth, on juftice, who has fix'd his throne :
    His face a thick tremendous darknefs fhrouds,   5
    His throne fupported by impervious clouds :
3 Confuming fire his prefence goes before,
    Whofe flames his haplefs enemies devour.
4 With his red forky lightning *æther* glares ;
    Stunn'd earth beholds ; fhe trembles and fhe fears :   10
5 At his appearance, ftruck with dread difmay,
    The lofty mountains melt, like wax, away ;
6 His righteous juftice heav'ns above declare ;
    The nations view his glory, and revere.
7 All they, who, loft in dull ftupidity,   15
    To fenfelefs gods of brafs have bow'd the knee,
    Shall meet confufion ; nay ; the gods ador'd
    Shall own almighty pow'r, and blefs the Lord.
8 And when dark errors clouds difperfe away,
    Shall *Sion* at the bleft event be gay ;   20
    When thou the fons of wickednefs deftroy,
    Shall *Judah*'s faithful daughters fing for joy ;
9 Far high above all heav'ns art thou, O Lord,
    Far higher than the fancied gods ador'd.
10 Therefore who truly love, who rev'rence thee,   25
    Shall keep their hearts from impious folly free ;
    For to the good thou art a conftant friend,
    And wilt their lives from ev'ry fnare defend ;
11 Thou on the righteous beam'ft a glorious light ;
    Beam'ft heav'nly joy on all that walk aright ;   30
12 Ye happy fouls, that tread the perfect way,
    In your good God your confidence difplay ;
    Grateful, in loud harmonious anthems, fing
    The mighty God, the univerfal king.

P S A L M

P S A L M *XCVIII.*

1 THE Lord *Jehovah* fing; in nobleft lays
  The wond'rous acts of your creator praife;
For why! a glorious conqueft he has gain'd
By his ftrong arm and by his mighty hand:
2 The nations all have felt his dreadful pow'r,   5
  The wicked joy, the righteous grieve, no more.
3 To *Ifrael's* tribes has he perform'd his word;
  Th' aftonifh'd *heathen* faw it, and ador'd.
4 Join then, all lands, in anthems to his name;
  Sing, fing our glorious God with loud acclaim: 10
5 The lute, the pfaltery, in his praife employ,
6 And let the clarion join the gen'ral joy.
7 Rejoice, thou fea, and all that in thee rove;
  Rejoice, thou earth, and all that in thee move:
8 Exult with gladnefs, all ye ftreaming floods;   15
  Exult with gladnefs, hills and lawns and woods.
9 For lo! he comes the righteous to reward;
  The righteous ever have his juft regard;
For lo! he comes his judgments to reveal,
And foon the wicked fhall his vengeance feel.   20

P S A L M *XCIX.*

1 REIGNS great *Jehovah*; let the people fear;
  Bright cherubs guard his throne; thou earth, revere:
2 Nor yet to *Sion* is his pow'r confin'd;
  Worlds feel the influence of *almighty mind.*
3 His great tremendous name they therefore praife,   5
4 The God with mercy and with truth, who fways;
  Whofe mercy ftrikes with love, whofe pow'r with awe,
  Who gives his favour'd tribes his perfect law:
5 Let all his dread omnipotence extol,
  And 'fore his footftool reverently fall.   10
6 When *Mofes* and the holy *Aaron* pray'd,
  When faithful *Samuel*, he lent his aid,
  His wond'rous goodnefs to them, gracious, fhew'd,
  And pointed to immortal blifs the road:
7 From out the cloudy pillar fpoke benign,   15
  (O bleft refult of clemency divine!)
  'Caufe, faithful, they his fov'reign will obey'd,
  Nor from the facred law he gave them, ftray'd.
8 Yes; thou, benignant father, deign'dft to hear,
  And, to the obdurate finner tho' fevere,   20

P   Indulgent

Indulgent ftill thine anfwers didft thou give,
And bad'ft the faithful in thy light to live.
9 For this, ye righteous fouls, with joint accord,
  Shout forth the praifes of your mighty Lord,
  And, 'caufe his glory there delights to dwell,   25
  Fall proftrate 'fore him on his holy hill.

P S A L M C.

1 YE nations all, howe'er difpers'd abroad,
    With voice united fing the living God;
2 With foul fincere his ftatutes all obey,
  And in glad anthems his bright pow'r difplay.
3 Our father, he-----he gave to nature birth,   5
  'Twas he that form'd us of the quicken'd earth;
  And ftill he fhews his kind paternal care,
  And feeds us fweetly in his paftures fair.
4 Therefore with joy let us his gate attend,
  And in his courts with grateful praifes bend,
  Own him our great creator and our king,   10
  And hymns harmonious to his glory fing.
5 For ever gracious, ever good, he'll prove;
  Unbounded his beneficence and love;
  Firm is his truth, inviolate his word-----
  To endlefs time protects the juft our Lord.   15

P S A L M CI.

1 OF mercy, Lord, of judgment, I will fing,
    Thy juftice and thy truth, eternal king;
2 This will I make my firm, my conftant rule,
  Still to improve in wifdom's facred fchool,
  Still on thy kind protection to depend,   5
  To keep my hands ftill clean, my heart unftain'd.
3 The ways of wickednefs I'll fcorn to view;
  The road thy law directs me, I'll purfue;
  The wily arts of fraudful men I'll hate,
  Of men who by oppreffion wou'd be great.   10
4 Far from my focial hours the froward be;
  The villain-herd fhall ne'er converfe with me;
5 By me the private fland'rer be abhorr'd,
  The cruel wretch that murders with a word;
  The haughty proud, whofe empty hearts are vain,   15
  Whofe looks are lofty, I alike difdain;

While

6 While men of open true fimplicity
  Shall to my converſe and my board be free;
  While men, who hate oppreſſion, fraud and wrong,
  Shall have my favour, and ſhall ſerve me long.   20

7 Avaunt, ye wicked, that deceive and lie,
  You're odious to my thought-----my preſence fly;

8 Yes; all ye impious, haſten quick away;
  Sure is my wrath, nor ſhall I long delay;
  Of all your guilt the city I will clear;   25
  Perdition waits you, and your fate is near.

P S A L M CII.

1 MY pleading cries, eternal father, hear,
    O lift, while I pour forth my mournful pray'r,

2 Nor from my griefs avert thy pitying eye;
  For deeply I'm o'erwhelm'd in miſery;
  Inceſſant woes my anguiſh'd ſoul invade;   5
  Propitious hear, and grant a ſpeedy aid.

3 Like ſmoak, like vapours, paſs my hours away;
  Griefs, like ſlow fires, upon my vitals prey;

4 Like wither'd graſs my ſmitten heart is grown,
  Like graſs that's wither'd by the ſcorching ſun;   10
  Faſt down my cheeks the ſcalding tears have flow'd,
  So that I've now no reliſh for my food;

5 My conſtant groans my body ſo conſume,
  That ſoon my ſhrivel'd corps will fill the tomb.

6 Juſt like the pelican that roves the wilds;   15
  Like the lone owl that in the deſart builds,
  Like the complaining dove that mourns her mate,
  Conſtant I wail, and brood upon my fate.

8 The bitter inſults of my foes I bear,
  While ſtill they baſely ſeek my life t' enſnare.   20

9 Tears make my drink, and aſhes are my bread,

10 'Cauſe threats thy fury my devoted head;
   'Cauſe, when from nought thou once hadſt rais'd me high,
   Plung'd by thy hand in deepeſt woe I lie.

11 Like a mere ſhadow fleets my life away,   25
   And my whole ſyſtem feels a ſwift decay.

12 But thou, O Lord, for ever art the ſame,
   And all our after-race ſhall hymn thy name;

13 Riſe then, bleſt father; bid thy love return;
   No more let *Sion* thy dread fury mourn;   30
   Riſe, and thy wonted clemency reſume,
   For ſure thy promis'd time to aid, is come.

P 2

See,

14 See, how all they, who love thy facred law,
   And hail thy name with reverential awe,
   Her fhatter'd walls, her broken tow'rs regret,
   And weep in pious tears her mournful fate.   35
15 Soon fhall the *heathen* realms thy pow'r proclaim,
   Soon earth's proud monarchs fear thy facred name;
16 When thou her ancient glory fhalt reftore;
   When fhe fhall wail thy heavy wrath no more;   40
17 When thou thy mournful fupplicants fhalt hear,
   And not, all-clement God, reject their pray'r.
18 This in eternal tablets fhall be writ,
   That times to come thy pow'r may not forget;
   That people yet unborn may give thee praife,   45
   And fing thy glory in immortal lays;
19 Gracious 'caufe thou from thy etherial throne
   Didft with an eye of love on man look down,
20 The fighs, the groans, of captive fouls didft hear,
   And freed'ft the death-devoted prifoner: 50
21 That *Sion*'s hill thy glory might refound,
   And *Salem* fing thy name to realms around,
22 While diftant nations croud thy facred dome,
   And fov'reign princes with their victims come.
23 Tho', while my race I run, my ftrength decays,   55,
   Tho' thou depriv'ft my life of half it's days;
24 To thee, O God, ftill fervently I'll pray;
   O take me not in my mid-age away;
   To everlafting time extend thy years;
25 Thy pow'r eternal in thy works appears,   60
   This earth, that fprung from nought at thy command,
   Yon heav'ns, the bright creation of thy hand.
26 They all fhall die, and, like a worn-out veft,
   Grow worfe by age, while thou'lt for ever laft;
   Great change, great alteration, fhall they feel,   65
27 While thou, great God, within thyfelf doft dwell,
   Eternally the fame; and doft difplay
   Thy pow'r to-day-----to-morrow-----yefterday.
28 Nay; e'en the faithful race, that worfhip thee,
   Have their bleft fhare in thy eternity;   70
   Tho' born in time, tho' creatures of thy hand,
   Immortal are their fouls, and have no end.

P S A L M *CIII.*

1 BE God of my harmonious fong the theme;
   His pow'r my ev'ry faculty proclaim;

And

2 And thou, my foul, his gracious works repeat)
   And not his great beneficence forget.

3 'Tis he, that all thy various crimes, forgives ;   5
   He diffipates thy pain when ficknefs grieves ;

4 With new-born vigour fortifies my mind,
   My life enlarges, and is ever kind.

5 From him each unexpected bleffing flows,
   His goodnefs 'bove my warmeft wifh beftows ;   10
   Renews my youth, that, like the eagle, ftrong,
   That fkims the azure plains, I'm ever young.

6 Juft his award-----when impious men opprefs,
   To him the injur'd 'plain, and meet redrefs.

7 He the meek *Mofes* taught his law divine,   15
   T' inftruct therein his *Ifrael's* favour'd line.

8 Gracious is he, and conftantly he gives,
   Slow is his wrath ; his mercy ever lives ;

9 And, if awhile our fins his anger raife,
   Soon he the fury of his wrath allays.   20

10 Great tho' our crimes, tho' daily we offend,
   Mild are his punifhments, and foon they end.

11. Farther than heav'n is from this earthly fphere,
   His goodnefs beams on all his name revere :

12 Wider than *eaft* from *weft* (fo much he loves   25
   The foul repentant) he our crimes removes.

13 As when a dear-lov'd child in duty fails,
   In the fond fire parental love prevails ;
   So, when offend the fervants he has chofe,
   From our good God forgiving mercy flows.   30

14 For well he knows the weaknefs of our frame,
   Well he remembers that from duft we came ;

15 As the green grafs, that for awhile looks gay,
   Then withers foon, fo paffes man away ;

16 Or like a blooming flow'r, whofe lovely pride   35
   Is by a cruel *fouthern* blaft deftroy'd.

17 But to the righteous fouls, their God that fear,
   And to their race, while they his will revere ;
   His juftice and his mercy ever lives,
   His juftice fhields them, and his love forgives ;   40

18 Keep they his ftatutes, and his laws obey,
   His goodnefs to them conftant he'll difplay.

19 High in yon ftarry heav'ns he 'as fix'd his throne,
   And o'er th' extended earth reigns Lord alone.

20 Ye fhining feraphs, ye celeftial bands,   45
   That hear his voice, and do his dread commands ;

Ye

Ye bright angelic hofts, that round him dwell,
In dignity, in beauty, who excell;
And all ye wond'rous works that fpeak his pow'r,
In hymns of harmony his name adore;　　　　　50
And thou, my foul, thou in the praife accord;
Blefs, blefs for ever the almighty Lord.

P S A L M　*CIV.*

1 THE nobleft fubject fwells my lofty lay,
　　　The Lord *Jehovah*-----I his pow'r difplay;
The Lord *Jehovah*, great creator-----God,
Who darts his dazzling glories all abroad;

2 Who's in tremendous majefty array'd,　　　　　5
With beamy light, as with a garment, clad:

3 Who, like a curtain, fpreads th' etherial plains;
In yon wide arch fufpends his fleecy rains,
By winds fupported, makes the clouds his car,
And rides triumphant in the ambient air.　　　　　10

4 Around him wait his bright angelic train,
Ready to bear his dread behefts to man;
Unbodied forms and effences divine
That fleet like *æther*, and like fire that fhine.

5 Firm on her bafe the folid earth he plac'd,　　　　　15
And 'gainft th' affaults of time fecur'd her faft;

6 The earth he cover'd with a watery flood;
High 'bove the loftieft hills the furges ftood;

7 But in tremendous thunder when he fpoke,
Soon they fubfided at his ftern rebuke;　　　　　20

8 The hills they leave, and feek the level plain,
And to their wonted depths return amain.

9 The bounds permitted them to pafs no more;
No more they on the delug'd mountains roar.

10 A long the vales, amid the tow'ring hills,　　　　　25
In fweet *meanders* flow the bubling rills;

11 Whence the wild beftials of the wildernefs,
And the rejoicing flocks, their thirft appeafe.

12 All on their margin, the aerial choir,
Whofe guilelefs loves their flender throats infpire,　　　　　30
Perch on the trees, and with their tuneful lay
Ravifh the plains, and cheat the ling'ring day.

13 Down from his ftores he fends his fruitful rains;
Feel their glad influence ftrait the meads, the plains;
All earth is ftrait with flow'rs, with herbage gay;　　　　　35

14 Rejoices man; the herds in rapture play;

The

The lovely profpect fills the heart with joy;
15 But what tranfporting ftrains our tongues employ,
When the fmooth oils around our temples fhine,
When high-enraptur'd with the racy wine;   40
When, by the bounty of our maker, fed,
New ftrength, new vigour, is fupplied by bread?
16 Nor lefs from him each vegetable tribe
Their fap receive-----th' enliv'ning juice imbibe
17 The tow'ring cedars where the eagles build,   45
The firs that to the ftorks fit refuge yield! —
18 The wanton goats along the mountains rove;
While the rough craggy cliff the coneys love.
19 He gives her ftated feafons to the moon;
He guides in his appointed courfe the fun;   50
20 His is the night; he bids the darknefs reign;
'Tis then the howling beftials range the plain;
Their haunts they leave, and by fell hunger led,
Fall on the flocks, and fill the fwains with dread.
21 Then the young lion with his hideous roar   55
Roams all abroad, the fatlings to devour;
To heav'n he roars, and while he prowls for food,
Owns, that his fole-dependence is on God.
22 But foon as e'er, with his reviving ray,
Comes forth the joyous fun, to gild the day,   60
The beftial-tribes all to their dens retreat,
23 And his alternate labours man await;
The live-long day in conftant toil he fpends,
Till kind indulgent night his travail ends.
24 Thy works, O God, difplay thy pow'r divine;   65
Thy glorious works proclaim, that wifdom's thine;
Nor earth alone thy mighty gifts can boaft;
25 The fea furvey'd, in wonder we are loft.
Such countlefs millions of the finny train,
That roam exulting o'er her glaffy plain;   70
Their different dimenfions who can trace?
The varied beauties of the fmaller race;
26 Th' enormous monfters, that with dreadful pride
Sport in the waves along the veffel's fide;
But moft, that dread, that huge *leviathan*,   75
The proud imperious tyrant of the main,
Who on her furface infolently plays,
And fills th' admiring eye with wild amaze.
27 O gracious God, all, all in fea, on land,
Receive their portion from thy mighty hand;   80

All,

All, all the bleſſings of thy bounty ſhare,
And all employ thy providential care.

28· Thou giv'ſt, they gather, their reſpective food ;
Thine hand thou open'ſt, and they're fill'd with good.

29 And, when thy glad'ning preſence is withdrawn,   85
The loſs of thy beneficence they mourn ;
Thou at thy pleaſure tak'ſt their breath away ;
They die, and ſtrait return to native clay.

30 Yet not without inhabitants the earth ;
Thy quick'ning ſpirit gives new forms a birth ;   90
A new creation ſprings ; their ſtated place
They hold, and run ſucceſſively their race.

31 Our God with glory ſhall for ever reign,
And will with joy his wond'rous works ſuſtain ;

32 Struck with his preſence, quakes the earth with fear ;   95
Mov'd at his dread rebuke the hills appear ;
See, from the hills in curling ſtreams ariſe
The circling ſmoak, and darken all the ſkies.

33 For me, while breath inſpires this vital frame,
The glories of my God ſhall be my theme ;   100
34 With joy ſincere his praiſes I will ſing,
And to his honour'd name attune the ſtring.

35 While impious men by his reſentment fall,
And direful woes their guilty hearts appall,
The great creator ſhall my ſoul inſpire,   105
Shall fill my tongue, and animate my lyre.

P S A L M *CV.*

1 SING to the Lord ; invoke his ſacred name ;
His glorious acts to all the earth proclaim ;
2 Our dread *Jehovah* claims your nobleſt lays ;
Loud let th' exulting tribes chant forth his praiſe.

3 Let his great name employ the grateful voice ;   5
Let all, that love his name, ſincere rejoice :
4 With firmeſt heart on his bleſt pow'r rely ;
His preſence aſk-----'twill ev'ry want ſupply.

5 Reflect the works of his almighty hand,
Th' obſervance that his ſacred laws command.   10
6 To you, bleſt *Abr'ham's* race, I ſpeak alone,
To you whom he hath deign'd to call his own.

7 He is our king, e'en he th' almighty God ;
Who to th' aſtoniſh'd earth his truth hath ſhew'd.
8 Firm to his covenant he 'as long remain'd,   15
Which for a thouſand ages he ordain'd ;

Which

9 Which he with *Abr'ham* made in days of yore,
  To which with *Isaac* solemnly he swore,
10 Which *Jacob* heard confirm'd, and which shall bless,
  Inviolate, to endless time, his race.   20
11 " To thee (he said) rich *Canaan*'s lands I'll give,
  " Thou in her fertile plains shalt ever live:"
12 E'en then, when yet they were but strangers there,
  And weak their pow'r, and few their numbers were ;
13 When they, as heav'n ordain'd, poor wand'rers, rov'd   25
  From place to place, and had no fix'd abode.
14 Yet them in peace his goodness still maintain'd ;
  The cruel rage of threat'ning kings restrain'd,
15 And bad them not those favour'd tribes oppress,
  Whom with peculiar love he chose to bless.   30
16 When a dire famine sore distrest the land,
  And scarce th' enfeebled nations life sustain'd,
17 Fair *Rachel*'s favour'd son he sent, a slave,
  To those glad lands, *Nile*'s fertile waters lave.
18 There long in prison, long in chains, he lay,   35
  'Til heav'n it's mercy to him did display,
19 Dreams to interpret, gave the wond'rous pow'r,
  And taught, the scheme of providence t' explore.
20 This heard the king; he set the pris'ner free,
  'Twas *Egypt*'s monarch gave him liberty.   40
21 He made a bond-slave ruler o'er his land ;
  O'er all the palace his was the command ;
22 That next in honour to his prince he stood,
  While all the nobles with obeisance bow'd.
23 'Twas then that *Israel* into *Egypt* came,   45
  And sojourn'd in the fruitful plains of *Ham*:
24 Our God his people 'bove the natives blest ;
  That soon in pow'r, in numbers, they increas'd.
25 This saw th' *Egyptian* monarch with regret,
  And strait fell on the favour'd tribes his hate :   50
26 Long suffer'd they, when their almighty friend
  Did humble *Moses* to their succour send.
27 *Aaron* and he by their dread wonders prove,
  That they had their commission from above.
28 Nature obeys, at once, their great command ;   55
  A gloomy darkness shrouds th' astonish'd land ;
29 Their streams polluted, flow with fetid gore,
  And all their fish lie dead upon the shore :
30 Not now the soil it's glad'ning produce yields,   60
  But frogs infest their palaces and fields.

Q

In

31 In fwarms unnumber'd rang'd the noifome flies,
　　And all their coafts are cover'd o'er with lice.
32 The kindly rains enrich their glebe no more,
　　But ftorms of hail and flame around them pour.
33 Their vines no more the chearful juice fupply,　　　65
　　And trees, fruits, flow'rs, in one wild ruin lie.
34 In flights the locufts and the beetles come,
　　And, what the hail hath left them, they confume;
　　So that not food for fuftenance remains,
　. But one wild defolation fills the plains.　　　　　70
36 Nay; more t' enhance their fatal miferies,
　　The favour'd fon, the dear-lov'd firft-born, dies.
37 At laft the humbled tyrant lets us go;
　　A joy fincere his ruin'd people fhew;
　　While we depart, of countlefs wealth poffeft,　　　75
　　With nervous ftrength, with fprightly vigour, bleft.
39 By a dun cloud he leads us in the day;
　　By night a glitt'ring fhine directs our way:
40 We afk, and ftrait we're fed with bread from heav'n;
　　We afk, and birds of richeft tafte are giv'n.　　-　80
41 The rock he fmote, and ftrait the waters came,
　　Free as a riv'let, gufh'd the flaking ftream.
42 For he his faithful *Abr'ham* not forgot,
　　Nor wou'd he bring his promifes to nought;
43 His gracious goodnefs pointed them the road;　　　85
　　With joy they follow'd their directing God.
44 The *heathen's* lands he gave them to poffefs;
　　And all the produce of their toils in peace;
45 That they his holy ftatutes might obey,　　-
　　And never from his dread commandments ftray.　　90

P S A L M   *CVI.*

1　WITH thankful hymns addrefs the mighty Lord;
　　　With fongs of joy be heav'n's high king ador'd;
　　For his beneficence to all extends;
　　His great, his glorious mercy never ends.
2 His wond'rous acts what eloquence difplays?　　　5
　　What tongue can utter all his pow'r, his praife?
3 Thrice happy they, that will his law obferve,
　　That love his law, nor from it's dictates fwerve!
4 Me with that gracious mercy view, O God,
　　Which to thy chofen thou haft conftant fhew'd;　　10
　　Look on me ftill with an indulgent eye,
5 That I thy people's bleffings may enjoy,

May long in their felicity rejoice,
And to thy glory tune my grateful voice.
6 Stiff and rebellious, like our fires, we prove,   15
And pay with bafe ingratitude thy love,
Plunge into horrid mifchiefs, and forget
How vaft thy pow'r, thy clemency how great;
7 So they, from hard, from cruel bondage freed,
Them to the fea when humble *Mofes* led,   20
Reflected not the wonders of thy hand,
Thy miracles in *Egypt*'s idol-land;
But, obftinately blind, in murmurs rofe
Againft the leader heav'n himfelf had chofe.
8 Yet his refentment ftill our God forbore;   25
That all might know and tremble at his pow'r;
9 He his dread mandate to the waters gave;
They heard, and ftrait fubfided ev'ry wave;
Erect they rofe-----he fpoke, and they obey'd-----
By his directing hand his people led,   30
10 Pafs o'er fecure, and gain the farther fhore,
And foon the rageful tyrant fear no more.
11 For, as the hoftile bands, refolv'd, purfue,
The waves returning on their ranks they view;
Whelm'd in the deep, they die-----not one remains;----- 35
12 But oh! amid the tribes what tranfport reigns?
How do they now believe? and how they praife
Their great Protector-God in thankful lays?
13 But all their dangers, all their fears remov'd,
Again rebellious to this God they prov'd;   40
Soon his ftupendous miracles forgot,
Nor on his pow'r, nor on his mercies thought.
14 Urg'd by their lufts, their murmurs foon they breathe,
Make infolent demands, and raife his wrath.
15 Their infolent demands they ftrait obtain'd;   45
Down from high heav'n the feather'd food he rain'd;
But while the cates the greedy tribes devour,
Adown their throats they fure perdition pour;
They eat and die-----provok'd, their angry God
With fatal fury, with dread vengeance glow'd.   50
16 But nought, when men are wilful in offence,
Avails or vengeance or beneficence;
Enflam'd with envy, ftill their murmurs rofe,
And *Mofes* and his brother they oppofe.
17 Their impious crimes dire punifhments await;   55
Her jaws earth opens, and devours them ftrait;

Q 2   *Confuming*

18 Confuming fire pours fudden from the fky,
   And all th' abettors and their race deftroy.
19 Still they're perverfe ; they now their Lord forfake,
   On *Horeb*'s mount an imag'd calf they make ;   60
   'Fore this they fall, and adoration pay ;
   Abfurd refemblance of what feeds on hay !
21 Ingrate ! their great redeemer to forget,
   How he fecur'd from bondage their retreat ;
22 What gracious mercies to them he had fhewn,   65
   What glorious wonders he had for them done.
23 'Twas then his dire refentment 'gainft them rag'd,
   Which had the faithful *Mofes* not affuag'd,
   Had he not ftood between their God and them,
   Extinct had been their race, and loft their name.   70
24 Sure now their harder'd hearts were ftruck with dread ;
   Sure now with eafe they by their chief were led ?
   Ah no ! by punifhment they're yet unaw'd,
   Again they murmur, and diftruft their God.
   Againft their leader and their God they rife ;   75
   Swift o'er the camp the winged tumult flies ;
   The joyous feats he promis'd them, they fcorn,
   And to his mercies make a bafe return.
26 Th' All-high, provok'd, rais'd then his mighty hand,
   Refolv'd to flay them in that defart land ;   80
27 To leave them to the nations round a prey,
   Deftroy their race, and fcatter them away.
28 Still obftinate, again they left their Lord,
   And *Baal*'s imag'd deity ador'd ;
   To him their victims and oblations paid,   85
   And bow'd before a mortal god for aid.
29 *Jehovah*, angry at this new offence,
   Sent on his tribes a deadly peftilence ;
   In *Baal*'s aid but poor relief they found ;
   Death, clad in all his horrors ftalk'd around ;   90
30 When *Phinehas* with divine refentment glow'd,
   And due regard for heav'n's high honour fhew'd ;
   The madnefs of the wretched croud reftrain'd,
   And a full refpite from their miferies gain'd :
   No more th' infection on their vitals prey'd,   95
   But by his ftrenuous arm the plague was ftay'd.
31 For this has he acquir'd a deathlefs name,
   And, long as lafts this earth, fhall live his fame.
32 And, *Meribah*, their guilt thy waters faw,
   When ftill the All-high's dread anger cou'd not awe   100

                                               Their

Their adamantine hearts; when still they shew'd
Their base distrust in their almighty God.
'Twas then, O *Moses*, that thy meekness fail'd;
Their constant murmurs o'er thy soul prevail'd; 105
Their base reproaches rais'd thy wrath too high,
And on this side of *Jordan* must thou die:

34 But sure, when of the promis'd land possest,
When with the fruitful fields of *Canaan* blest,
Their God they worshipp'd and his will obey'd,
And never from the law he gave them stray'd? 110
Ah! still his dread behests they durst withstand,
And not destroy'd the natives of the land:

35 But, to their base idolatries inclin'd,
36 Soon in their impious rites with them they join'd;
Of fancied deities they sought th' abodes, 115
And offer'd human victims to their gods:

37 Nay; their own infants (horrid is the thought)!
Unnatural parents to their demons brought;
Around their altars stream'd the vital flood,
And all the sacred land's distain'd with blood. 120

39 Thus they the aid of fancied gods implor'd;
Thus they the works of their own hands ador'd.
40 Therefore the Lord with dreadful fury burn'd;
Justly the people he had chose, he scorn'd;
41 He to the nations gave them up a prey, 125
And they their most invet'rate foes obey.
42 Their lordly foes with insolence oppress,
And load them with the most severe distress.
43 And yet, if e'er their gracious God reliev'd,
Still their obdurate hearts his spirit griev'd; 130
Still to their wonted crimes wou'd they return,
His name reject, and at his statutes spurn.
44 Yet still his mercy and his goodness sway'd;
Oft he reliev'd them, when they sought his aid;
45 Oft mindful of his covenant he prov'd, 135
Forgave their crimes, and all their woes remov'd.
46 And, when for their impieties brought low,
They bore th' oppressions of the haughty foe,
With soft compassion he the conqu'ror struck,
That still more mild, more gentle, was the yoke. 140
47 O sov'reign Lord, thy favour'd tribes defend;
Still 'gainst the *heathen* be our pow'rful friend;
That we thy wond'rous glory may proclaim,
And sing in grateful hymns thy holy name:

That

48 That *Ifrael*'s race may *Ifrael*'s God extol,   145
    And, while this earth fhall live, on thee may call ;
    Thy pow'r, thy might, thy majefty, may fing,
    And hail their gracious God, their heav'nly king.

P S A L M   *CVII.*

1 FOR ever lafts the mercy of the Lord ;
    His name in pious anthems be ador'd ;
2 Yes ; praife him, all, who from th' oppreffor's chain
    Have afk'd redemption, and not afk'd in vain.
    Whom, when with cruel hate their foes diftreft,   5
    His gracious goodnefs with deliv'rance bleft.
3 From all the various corners of the earth
    With his directing hand he led them forth ;
4 Long in the lonely defart did they roam,
    Nor knew the path to their appointed home ;   10
5 Fainting with thirft, quite deftitute of food,
    What complicated woes their fteps purfued ?
    The defart wilds no kind repaft fupplied ;
    To flake their thirft, the cooling ftream denied.
6 'Twas in this fore diftrefs to heav'n they pray'd,   15
    And heav'n in mercy haften'd to their aid ;
7 Led them the way to opulence and peace,
    And gave them lands and cities to poffefs.
8 Then let them fing their good, their gracious God,
    And publifh his beneficence abroad :   20
9 For food he gives, and all our griefs controuls,
    Strengthens our limbs, and fatisfies our fouls.
10 Who, vain, rejected dread *Jehovah*'s law,
    Nor heard his word with reverential awe,
11 When in the confines of the grave they lay,   25
    O'erwhelm'd in darknefs, funk in dire difmay ;
12 When ills inceffant wrung their hearts with pain,
    And death came ftalking with his meagre train ;
13 In their diftrefs to heav'n they earneft pray'd,
    And heav'n in mercy haften'd to their aid ;   30
14 Bad all the terrors of their fouls to ceafe,
    Broke off their fetters, and reftor'd their peace.
15 Then let them fing their good, their gracious God,
    And publifh his beneficence abroad ;
16 He to the captive liberty enfures,   35
    Unbinds his chains, and breaks the prifon-doors.
17 By lures of fenfe when men are led aftray,
    And the foul dictates of their luft obey,

They

They feel th' inflictions of his heavy wrath;
Some dire diftemper draws them nigh to death :   40
They relifh now their luxuries no more ;
And loath the dear-bought cates they priz'd before.
19 But if in their diftrefs to heav'n they pray,
His mercy drives the foul difeafe away,
20 Heals all their pains, bids new-born vigour rife,   45
And firms their fouls-----the dreaded fpectre flies.
21 Let fuch fing then the goodnefs of their God,
And publifh his beneficence abroad ;
22 With victims croud his facred courts, and fing
Glad hymns of praife to their all-clement king.   50
23 Who plough the furface of the raging main,
And dare the fury of her waves for gain,
24 To them his dread tremendous works appear;
They view his wonders in the deep with fear.
25 At his command the ftormy winds arife,   55
And raife her foamy billows to the fkies :
26 High as the heav'ns his waves old *ocean* rears ;
Aloft they mount, and feem to threat the ftars ;
Then fudden to the depths below fubfide,
And in the horrible abyfs are hid.   60
27 What terrors then the mariners affail,
What killing fears o'er their fad hearts prevail,
When, like a wretch o'erpower'd with wine, they reel,
And the toft veffel mocks the mafter's fkill ?
28 But, if to heav'n in their diftrefs they pray,   65
He drives their dangers and their fears away,
29 Calls off his winds, and ftrait allays the ftorm ;
Still are th' obedient waves ; the fea grows calm ;
30 The mariners rejoice, their terrors o'er,
And the torn bark fcuds fwiftly to the fhore.   70
31 Let fuch fing then their good, their gracious God,
And publifh his beneficence abroad.
32 Yes ; all ye people, all, his pow'r proclaim,
And in the great affemblies hail his name ;
33 'Tis he forbids the flood t' enrich the lands,   75
And turns the living fprings to barren fands ;
34 'Tis he, when rages wickednefs around,
Curfes with quick fterility the ground ;
35 He too the defart wilds with water fills,
And bleffes thirfty foils with fruitful rills ;   80
No more their wonted barrennefs they mourn,
But foon look gay with herbage, fruits and corn.

Thefe

36 Thefe to induftrious poverty he gives;
 The colony, by him fupported, thrives;
 Their wives, their infants, ftrong-built towns defend;   85
37 Their tilth with joy the painful farmers tend;
 They fow the grain, they plant the fruitful vine,
 That foon repays their toil with gen'rous wine.
38 Their God looks o'er them with protectful eye,
 Hears all their pray'rs, does ev'ry want fupply;   90
 With a fair off-fpring crowns their chafte embrace,
 And gives of cattle the defir'd increafe.
39 But, when, elated with their profp'rous fate,
 The mercies of the donor they forget,
 They heav'ns beneficence no more engage,   95
 But feel the fury of almighty rage:
40 He gives them up to tyranny a prey,
 They foon fome proud imperious prince obey;
 Their prince and they are equally a fcorn
 To realms around, and their contempt they mourn;   100
 Stript of their wealth, they roam wild defarts o'er,
 Where human feet have never trod before.
41 Yet ftill the humble and the modeft mind
 A fure protection in his love fhall find;
 Secure from ills, by him they're fet on high,   105
 Rewarded with a num'rous progeny.
42 This view the righteous, and fincere rejoice,
 And to his glory tune the grateful voice;
 While impious finners fullenly repine,
 And mock in gloomy filence truth divine.   110
43 Whoe'er is wife, and on the bleft effects
 Of heav'n's high juftice ferioufly reflects,
 Will know, and own, that mercy, truth and love,
 Pertain to him alone, who rules above.

P S A L M *CVIII.*

1 FIX'D is my heart; my heart's refolv'd, O God,
 To fpread thy glory, and thy praife abroad;
2 Awake, my lyre-----my pfaltery-----my voice-----
 At early dawn I'll in my God rejoice;
3 My fong of thee the nations round fhall hear,
 And, with the theme tranfported, thee revere.
4 For to yon tracklefs clouds, yon heav'ns above
 Extend thy truth, thy clemency, thy love.
5 Do thou, O God, exalt thy glory high;
 Beam on th' aftonifh'd earth thy majefty;   10

O

6 O fave the pious foul that trufts in thee, _
  And with thy mighty arm thy fervant free.

7 But fpeaks our God-----hear all his awful words;
  (What folemn joy his heav'nly voice affords)!
  " Fair *Shechem*'s fertile fields thy lot fhall be;
  " I'll mete out *Succoth*'s lovely vales for thee.   15

8 " The faithful tribes of *Ifrael*, ar'n't they mine,
  " To me confirm'd by fanctions moft divine?

9 " Therefore their great protector I'll be found;
  " Therefore for them I'll curb the nations round;   20
  " I'll lay them all beneath their conqu'ring feet;
  " *Idume*, *Moab*, *Paleftine*, fubmit."

10 Who to yon lofty town the path will fhew?
  To *Edom*'s tow'ring gates our leader who?

11 Say, wilt not thou, O God, tho' in thy wrath   25
  Thou'ft caft us off, and threatened us with death?
  Say, wilt not thou, tho' late thine anger rofe,
  And thou not led'ft us 'gainft our haughty foes?

12 But now, dread father, thy affiftance give,
  For vain are human aids----they but deceive.   30

13 Our leader thou, intrepidly we'll fight,
  We'll conquer and we'll triumph in thy might;
  Our leader thou, our haughty foes fhall bleed,
  And on their humbled necks we'll joyous tread.

P S A L M CIX.

1 STRICT filence keep not, fov'reign Lord-----behold,
     How impious men in horrid guilt are bold;

2 What fraudful fnares againft my foul they fcheme,
  In what calumnious terms they blaft my name.

3 'Gainft me in caufelefs hatred they engage,   5
  And afk my life the victim of their rage:

4 My proffer'd love, my friendfhip they oppofe,
  And, 'caufe I'd be their friend, become my foes;
  Their hearts fuch vile ingratitude has fway'd,
  With bafe returns my favours they repay'd.   10
  Howe'er in pray'r to thee I folace find,
  To thee who know'ft each fecret of my mind.

6 But give o'er him fome cruel prince command,
  Let fome dire demon at his elbow ftand;

7 If 'fore the dread tribunal he appear,   15
  Trembling, let him th' impartial fentence hear;
  The mercy of his judge may he intreat
  In vain, and may his pray'r but irritate.

R   Few

 8 Few be his days, and fudden may he bleed,
   And let a ftranger to his home fucceed;   20
 9 May his 'lorn widow and his orphan-race
   Be vagabonds, and roam from place to place,
10 Beg for their bread, yet not receive relief,
   Nor one kind friend commiferate their grief;
11 While bafe extortioners his goods poffefs,   25
   And heirs unknown on all his treafures feize.
12 May he and may his children plead in vain
   ·For mercy, and may all their fuit difdain;
13 Nay; let his progeny be all deftroy'd,
   Sunk be his name, and his memorial void.   30
14 Remember, Lord, th' offences of his fire,
   And let his mother's guilt increafe thine ire;
15 Their ev'ry crime thy piercing eyes explore,
   Till earth fhall hear their curfed names no more.
16 For he the needy never wou'd relieve,   35
   Nor to th' afflicted kind affiftance give;
   From their petitions turn'd his face away,
   And call'd it joy the guilelefs foul to flay.
17 As curfing was his dear, his fole delight,
   On his own head his imprecations light;   40
   As never from his tongue a bleffing fell,
   Let none e'er give him joy, or wifh him well.
18 As he his foul with curfes has array'd,
   May they, like oil, his very bones pervade,
   Into his bowels, fwift as waters, ftream,   45
   And the whole man with deadly pangs enflame;
19 Their dire effects O may he ever feel,
   Nor have it in his pow'r their wounds to heal.
20 Be this, juft God, their lot, that harafs me,
   And vex my foul with cruel calumny.   50
21 But me, great God, thy goodnefs ftill defend,
   And for thy mercy's fake be ftill my friend;
22 For poor I am; in fore diftrefs I lie;
   Deep am I wounded; heavily I figh:
23 Like a mere fhadow on a fummer's day,   55
   Weak and infirm, my fubftance wears away;
   Toft to and fro, in devious paths I rove,
   Like locufts ranging o'er the leafy grove.
24 My feeble limbs their wonted aid refufe,
   And all my beauty, all my ftrength, I lofe: 60
25 My foes with proud difdain my peace invade,
   And, fcornful, fhake at my diftrefs the head.

                                        But

26 But save me, Lord, and let thy servant live;
　O let thy mercy plead; sweet solace give;
27 That all may know, thy hand defends my cause, 　　　65
　My soul her solace from thy goodness draws:
28 With bitter imprecations while they foam,
　On me the blessings of thy mercy come;
　While dire confusion all their peace destroy,
　O fill my faithful heart with solid joy. 　　　70
29 Let them who load with calumnies my fame,
　Be with dishonour cloath'd, and lost in shame.
30 Then to my God my grateful voice I'll raise,
　And in the throng'd assemblies hymn thy praise;
31 Sing, how the poor are objects of thy love, 　　　75
　How thou their strength, their great support, wilt prove;
　How thou reliev'st them in their dire distress,
　And shield'st their pious souls, when foes oppress.

P S A L M CX.

1 THUS to our *Christ* the Lord *Jehovah* said;
　(Shook as he spoke th' etherial worlds with dread);
　" At my right hand, my best-beloved, sit,
　" Till all thine enemies shall kiss thy feet.
2 " From *Sion*'s hill to earth's extremest shore, 　　　5
　" The rod I'll send, the emblem of thy pow'r;
　" That 'mid the nations thou may'st hold the sway,
　" And thy rebellious foes thy rule obey.
3 " In joyous pomp, when thou shalt back return,
　" And conquest's splendid meed thy head adorn; 　　　10
　" The people shall attend with loud acclaim,
　" Shall celebrate thy deeds, and hail thy name;
　" Thick as the spangles on the dewy plain,
　" Shall swarm the nations, and assert thy reign.
4 " By his dread self th' almighty Godhead swore; 　　　15
　" (And ne'er shalt thou his broken oath deplore)
　" That thou the royal priesthood long shalt share,
　" And great *Melchizedek*'s high office bear;
　" Long as shall beam the sun his glad'ning light;
　" Long as the waining moon illumes the night. 　　　20
5 " At thy right-hand shall ever stand the Lord,
　" And strike fell tyrants with his flaming sword;
6 " The impious nations all shall feel his wrath,
　" He dooms their proud rebellious chiefs to death;
7 " As he pursues, the riv'let in his way 　　　25
　" Offers it's stream, his fiery thirst t' allay;

Then

" Then crown'd with conqueft, ftrait he lifts on high
" His glorious head, and emulates the fky.

P S A L M *CXI.*

1 WITH me, ye varied nations, hymn your God ;
  On me while life, while vig'rous health's beftow'd,
  With heart fincere his wond'rous works I'll fing,
  And 'mid the tribes chant our all-clement king.
2 Great are his works-----who with a humble mind   5
  Surveys them, foon their excellence will find.
3 O'er all his works a majefty divine,
  A bright refulgent glory conftant fhine ;
  O'er all his works, while glads yon fun the plains,
  Mankind fhall own impartial juftice reigns.   10
4 The wonders he in days of yore hath wrought,
  His mighty acts, fhall never be forgot:
  His mercy hears the wretched in their grief,
  Compaffionates their woes, and grants relief.
5 The righteous fouls, that have his will purfued,   15
  From him have been fupplied with daily food :
  His faith his people never fhall upbraid,
  For long he'll keep the covenant he made.
6 By the illuftrious deeds his hand hath done,
  To them his dread omnipotence is fhewn :   20
  He drove the *heathen* from their fruitful plains,
  And bleft his people with their rich domains.
7 Juftice and truth o'er all his works prefide ;
  His dread right-hand ftrict truth and juftice guide ;
  His bleft commands the ftrongeft bafis have,   25
  By truth, by juftice, he delights to fave ;
8 For ever firm, th' affaults of time are vain,
  'Gainft them, and they for ever fhall remain.
9 In bondage moft fevere when *Ifrael* figh'd,
  And to their God in bitter anguifh cried ;   30
  He not delay'd his favour'd tribes to free,
  But promis'd them continued liberty,
  If from the paths of juftice they'd not ftray,
  But to his law a due attention pay ;
  For reverend and holy is his name,   35
  And ftrict obedience to his law he'll claim.
10 And fure t' obferve the ftatutes of our God,
  To heav'nly wifdom is the certain road ;
  By this fure rule who guides his fteps, will find
  Unftain'd his confcience, and illum'd his mind ;   40
                                                       And,

And, while this earth, and while yon heav'ns-shall last,
Those, that are truly wife, pronounce him blest.

P S A L M _CXII._

1 THRICE blest the man, that great _Jehovah_ fears,
  Observes his law, and his dread will reveres !
2 In honour long his progeny shall live ;
 And 'mong the nations great respect receive :
3 His life he spends in peace, in wealth, in pow'r,   5
 His name will last, when he himself's no more :
4 While fore distresses wicked men confound,
 Our God will beam his light the just around ;
 For, ever gracious, ever good, he frees,
 The pious foul from woe, and gives her ease.   10
5 The good man's bountiful, and constant gives,
 And injur'd innocence with joy relieves ;
 And, with discretion while his life he guides,
 His wealth he with the indigent divides.
6 " No storms of fate his steady foul can move," 15
 His foul, that fcorns the earth, and foars above :
 Ne'er dark oblivion can involve his name,
 Nor time itself obliterate his fame.
7 No dismal tidings can his heart surprize ;
 Firm is his heart, and on his God relies ;   20
8 Firm as a rock, he dares his threat'ning foes,
 For heav'n himself his sure support he knows.
9 The wealth that he with chearfulness bestow'd,
 The kind compassion to the poor he shew'd,
 His merit and his glory high will raise,   25
 And propagate his name to after-days.
10 This views the wicked with indignant eye ;
 Rank spite and envy all his peace destroy ;
 He chafes, he frets, he pines, the live-long day,
 And with unbated malice wastes away.   30

P S A L M _CXIII._

1 YOUR maker's praise, ye righteous souls, proclaim ;
  All ye his servants, hymn his holy name ;
2 The name of your tremendous Lord adore,
 That all to endless time may hail his pow'r ;
3 From morn to night, while glads the fun the day, 5
 Let man the mercies of his God display ;

His

4 His God, above the nations feated high,
  High in the heav'ns, enthron'd in majefty.
5, What fancied god can with our God compare ?
  Whofe throne's fupported by the azure air ;   10
6 Whofe eye, all-feeing, heav'n and earth pervades,
7 Who in their deep diftrefs the wretched aids ;
8 The poor who raifes from his low eftate,
  And, equal with proud princes, makes him great ;
9 Who gives the fterile womb a fruitful birth ;   15
  With joy the matron brings her iffue forth ;
  With joy fhe views her progeny around ;
  -----The praifes of your God, ye juft, refound.

P S A L M *CXIV.*

1 WHEN *Ifrael* to their native fields return'd,
    And left the barb'rous lands, where long they 'ad
2 Their God protectful led them in the way,   [mourn'd,
  And o'er their camp his banners did difplay :
3 The troubled fea beheld him, and fhe fled ;   5
  Flow'd back th' affrighted *Jordan* to his head ;
4 The lofty hills from their foundations mov'd ;
  Like fportive flocks along the plains, they rov'd.
5 What faw the fea, that fhe fo fudden fled ?
  Why roll'd his ftreams ftunn'd *Jordan* to his head ?   10
6 Why did the hills from their foundations move ?
  Why, like the flocks, along the paftures, rove ?
7 Why ? 'Caufe all earth was at his prefence aw'd,
  And trembled when fhe faw th' almighty God ;
8 Who turn'd the rock into a living ftream,   15
  Who gave the word, and ftrait the waters came.

P S A L M *CXV.*

1 NOT to ourfelves, O God, we afk a name,
    Nor want to glitter in the lifts of fame ;
  To our own honour we'd no trophies raife ;
  Be thine the glory, and be thine the praife.
2 Why fhou'd the *heathen* fpread their taunts abroad,   5
  And afk infulting, Where is now your God ?
3 Where is our God ? 'Bove yon bright worlds on high,
  With glory all-array'd, with majefty ;
  His boundlefs pow'r o'er all the earth is known ;
  His pow'r with dire difmay they foon fhall own ;   10
                                                           Shall

4 Shall prove the weaknefs of the faith they hold
In imag'd gods, of filver, and of gold ;
In gods, who not their pray'rs can underftand,
But owe their being to the fculptor's hand.
5 A mouth they have ; yet have they not a voice ;   15
Have eyes, yet cannot in the light rejoice ;
6 Their noftrils no rich fragrant odours tafte,
Nor with harmonious found their ears are bleft ;
7 Their hands are ufelefs, and their feet not move ;
Speech is not theirs-----what peerlefs gods they prove ?   20
8 Bright objects of devotion's holy flame,
And wife are they, fuch deities who frame,
And wifer ftill, beyond defcription wife,
The man, who, on the god he makes, relies !
9 But thou, O *Ifrael*, truft thou in the Lord,   25
And he'll to thee his fureft aid afford ;
10 Ye houfe of *Aaron*, on your God rely,
And in diftrefs affiftance he'll fupply ;
11 Croud, croud, ye pious fouls, his facred court,
For he'll the righteous conftantly fupport.   30
12 Still mindful of his people, ftill he'll blefs,
And crown their days with affluence and peace.
13 Or be they young, or old, or rich, or poor,
They have his favour, who his name adore ;
14 The happy objects of his love they are,   35
And e'en their children's children prove his care.
15 Who form'd yon heav'ns and this terreftrial ball,
Benignly hears us, and preferves us all.
16 The heav'ns with his own prefence does he grace,
And gives this beauteous earth to human race.   40
17 While not the filent dead their maker praife,
18 We'll chant his glory in fublimeft lays ;
While rolls this fpacious globe, our God we'll fing,
And hymn for ever our immortal king.

P S A L M *CXVI.*

1 THE mighty God I'll love with heart unfeign'd ;
To him in vain I never yet complain'd ;
2 He to my mournings lent a gracious ear ;
'Fore him I'll therefore breathe my ardent pray'r.
3 In killing griefs, in deep diftrefs, I lay ;   5
Death with his horrid train befet my way ;
I on the verge of dire deftruction ftood,
4 When loudly I implor'd my gracious God ;

O

" O fov'reign Lord, my anguifh'd foul relieve,
" Difperfe my woes, and let me ceafe to grieve."   10
5 How good our God! how ready to relieve!
6 My woes difpers'd, he bad me ceafe to grieve.
7 Therefore fhall I my wonted 'plaints forbear,
Since not unworthy of Almighty care;
8 Since he of threat'ning death hath calm'd my fears,   15
From my full eyes has wip'd away the tears,
My feet hath ftrengthen'd, that I firmly tread,
9 No more the terrors of the grave I dread;
But fafe in his protecting love, I fing
His praife, and to his glory ftrike the ftring.   20
10 Sad was my foul, in deep affliction loft,
In fears of my impending dangers toft;
11 " On man 'tis fruitlefs to rely (I faid)
" But heav'n is fure, if heav'n will give his aid."
12 His aid he gave; he drove my griefs away;   25
And how fhall I his clemency repay?
13 With rich libations I'll my God adore,
And hail in hymns of pious joy his pow'r;
14 My victims fhall his hallow'd courts attend,
And 'mid th' affemblies 'fore his throne I'll bend;   30
15 For precious in his fight the righteous are,
He frees their fouls from death, their lives from care;
16 Me from my bonds did he relieve, and fave
His finking fervant from the gaping grave.
17 Therefore with thankful heart 'fore him I'll fall,   35
And on his honour'd name devoutly call;
18 Amid his people I my vows will pay,
Hafte to his facred dome without delay,
My victims fhall his facred courts attend,
And his great name I'll praife, till time fhall end.   40

P S A L M *CXVII.*

1 YE nations all, howe'er difpers'd, proclaim
Your maker's praife, and hymn his holy name;
2 His goodnefs and his clemency relate;
Own, that your God is ever good, as great;
That firm his truth, inviolate his word-----   5
Ye fcatter'd nations, hymn the living Lord.

P S A L M

P S A L M CXVIII.

1 OUR fov'reign Lord, the great *Jehovah* praife,
   Ye tribes, of *Abr'ham* the diftinguifh'd race ;
Bleft *Aaron*'s fons, that at his altar bow ;
Ye juft, whofe fouls with heav'nly fervour glow ;
Sing, fing our fov'reign Lord in loftieft ftrains,
And own, his clemency for ever reigns.

5 To him in dire calamity I pray'd ;
  My voice he heard, and gave a fpeedy aid.

6 And he my help, while he my caufe fuftains,
  My foul the threats of haughty man difdains ;

7 And he my help, I'll on that help rely,
  While direful ruin ftrikes the enemy.

8 'Tis fafer far in his ftrong arm to truft,
  Than in the boafted ftrength of feeble duft ;

9 On our great God 'tis fafer to depend,
  Than have earth's mightieft monarch for our friend.

10 Me tho' the nations all around affail,
  I'll in th' affiftance of his hand prevail ;

11 Let them e'en with their utmoft force affail ;
  -----His mercy aids-----his *David* muft prevail ;

12 Tho' round me their broad banners they difplay,
  And fwarm like bees upon a fummer's day,
  By him fupported, on their ranks I'll fly,
  And, fpite of numbers, fnatch the victory.

13 All your attempts, ye wicked, are in vain ;
  The mighty God his fervant will fuftain ;

14 He is my ftrength, the fubject of my lay,
  My great falvation he, my prop, my ftay ;

15 The righteous all in my fuccefs rejoice,
  And to *Jehovah*'s glory tune the voice ;

16 Sing his ftrong arm, and his refiftlefs hand,
  His arm, that crouded ranks in vain withftand ;
  His valiant hand, that ftrikes the deadly blow,
  And pours fevere deftruction on the foe.

17 Fruitlefs thy infults, death ;-----thy fhafts I dare ;
  Long fhall I live, and heav'n's high pow'r declare ;

18 True ; long his fad afflicting hand I bore ;
  Yet ftill he fav'd me from thy ruthlefs pow'r.

19 Ope wide, ye holy priefts, his temple-gate,
  That I may there his wond'rous works relate ;

20 The gate by him belov'd, where wait the juft,
  To fhew in him their confidence and truft.

21 Thee, gracious God, I'll praife, for in my grief
  My voice thou heard'ft, and gav'ft a quick relief.

S

22 Me from the rageful foe didſt thou protect ;
 The ſtone which late the builders did reject, 45
'High in the lofty fabric now is plac'd,
And ſhines conſpicuous, far above the reſt:

23 So wills th' almighty Lord ; and what he wills,
Our ſouls with wonder and with rapture fills. 50

24 Hail, happy day! hail, bright refulgent morn!
That to the joy of all the earth wilt dawn!

25 Still favour, Lord, the king thou haſt ordain'd ;
Bring all his efforts to a glorious end:

26 Thrice happy he, whom thou ſhalt ſend, to bleſs 55
Thy favour'd people with eternal peace!
Succeſs attend him!-----this the pray'r of all,
That 'fore thy altar reverently fall.

27 For thou art God, the only pow'r divine ;
Thou bid'ſt thy glory on thy tribes to ſhine ; 60
Hear this, ye righteous, and loud anthems ſing ;
And to his hallow'd dome your victims bring.

28 With heart, with voice, my God, will we adore
Thy name, and ſing thy praiſe, till time's no more:

29 Praiſe all *Jehovah* in ſublimeſt ſtrains ; 65
To all eternity his mercy reigns.

˙P S A L M   *CXIX.*

A L E P H.

1 **T**HRICE happy they, who with religious awe,
  With pureſt hearts, obſerve God's ſacred law!

2 The way their maker teaches, who purſue,
And to the dictates of his word are true!

3 Such will from ev'ry heinous crime be clear ; 5
They keep the ſtatutes of their God in fear.

4 For 'tis his will, that ſtrictly we obey
His bleſt commands, and never from them ſtray.

5 O that my ways were order'd ſo aright,
That I might ſhew therein my high delight! 10

6 If from thy precepts I forbore to part,
No ſhame wou'd ſeize my ſoul, no grief my heart ;

7 Thy judgments when I 'ad learn'd, with conſcience gay
Thy righteous juſtice gladly I'd diſplay:

8 Yes, Lord, thy law my conſtant rule I'd make ; 15
------O not thy ſervant utterly forſake.

B E T H.

9 How ſhall a young man well his conduct guide?
-----When heav'n's high laws o'er all his ſteps preſide.

10 So have I ever found-----ftill, gracious God,
   Still let me keep the fame unerring road.   20

11 Thy word my conftant inmate, Lord, hath been
   To guard me from the fatal lures of fin.

12 Moft worthy thou of praife-----preferve me ftill
   In due obedience to thy facred will:

13 That on thy law I yet may meditate;   25
   That yet my tongue thy judgments may relate.

14 Not wealth, not honours, 'fuch true pleafure give
   As from my firm obedience I receive.

15 Therefore thy precepts fill my inmoft thought,
   My foul to rev'rence them is daily taught;   30

16 Thy laws to me fincereft joy afford,
   And I'll ne'er flight the dictates of thy word.

G I M E L.

17 To me the bleffings of thy grace impart,
   That ftill thy ftatutes may direct my heart;

18 With thy effectual light illume my mind,   35
   That fhe the wonders of thy law may find;

19 On earth but as a fojourner I dwell;
   Thou not thy precepts from my foul conceal.

20 My foul that fickens with defire to know
   The facred laws that from thy wifdom flow.   40

21 O thou, that, when the wicked wilful err,
   Rebuk'ft their pride, and ftrik'ft their hearts with fear,

22 Since faithful to thy dread commands I prove,
   From me contempt and calumny remove.

23 The great ones of the earth againft me fpeak,   45
   'Caufe I thy ftatutes refolutely feek;

24 Their obloquy I fcorn-----thy ftatutes ftill
   Shall guide my heart, and regulate my will.

D A L E T H.

25 Droops my fad foul; fhe languifhes in grief;
   Do thou, as thou haft promis'd, grant relief;   50

26 The fecrets of my heart I've not conceal'd,
   But ev'ry error of my life reveal'd.

27 O let me then thy precepts underftand;
   And fing the wonders of thy mighty hand.

28 With pain, with anguifh, melts my foul away;   55
   But thou thy mercy in her cure difplay.

29 Let me, my lips from falfhood to refrain,
   A perfect knowledge in thy precepts gain.

30 The ways of truth, of juftice, I have chofe,
   And thy bleft judgments as my rule propofe;   60

31 Thy law the pleafure of my life I've made,
   Let not reproach my guilelefs foul upbraid:

S 2

If

32 If thou my heart from all her cares wilt free,
   I'll ever tread the path preſcrib'd by thee.
H E.

33 Give me, the way of thy commands to know;   65
   The *ſalutary* road unto me ſhew;
   Them to obſerve, my utmoſt ſoul I'll bend,
   And keep the road till life itſelf ſhall end.

35 Yes; in thy ſtatutes is my high delight;
   O guide me, lead me, that I walk aright.   70

36 Deaf may I prove to avarice's call,
   And never in the ſnares of folly fall;
   But to thy precepts thou my heart incline;
   And ſtill ſupport me with thy pow'r divine.

38 Thy ſervant firmly on thy word relies,   75
   He owns, thy judgments all are good, are wiſe;
   Long let him prove thy providential care,
   Nor the vile calumnies of ſcoffers bear.

40 Thy law, thy precepts, will he conſtant love,
   May he thy favour and thy mercy prove.   80
V A U.

41 Be mindful of thy covenant, O Lord;
   Support my ſoul, as promiſes thy word;

42 That, when the wicked with their taunts aſſail,
   I may 'gainſt their opprobrious wrongs prevail.

43 Truth let me ever ſpeak, and ſcorn a lie;   85
   For to thy juſtice for defence I fly.

44 So, long as breath inſpires this vital clay,
   Thy law ſhall I effectually obey;

45 So, in the paths of ſafety I ſhall tread,
   Still live in peace, and no miſfortunes dread: 90

46 Thy law, thy ſtatutes, fearleſs, I'll aver;
   Thy law e'en ſceptre'd kings from me ſhall hear;

47 Obedience to thy law my ſole employ,
   Thy law I'll make my only, conſtant joy:

48 Thy law I've ever lov'd, and ſtill will love,   95
   And nought on earth my fix'd reſolve ſhall move.
Z A I N.

49 Remember, Lord, the promiſe thou haſt made;
   'Tis on that promiſe I rely for aid;

50 My conſolation this in deep diſtreſs;
   Thy word conſoles me, when my foes oppreſs.   100

51 For, when the proud with baſe deriſion wound,
   Bleſt comfort in thy love I've ever found.

52 Of old thy judgments I have ne'er forgot;
   And they have chear'd my ſoul, and eas'd my thought:
And,

53 And, tho' with horror I the wicked view,   105
   And grieve to fee the meafures they purfue;
54 Yet in this vale of mis'ry while I ftay,
   Thy law fhall be the fubject of my lay.
55 At night fweet folace in thy law I find,
   E'en in the gloom thy name relieves my mind;   110
56 Or night or day 'tis my continued care,
   Thy name to fing, thy ftatutes to declare.

C H E T H.

57 My portion thou, my hope, my wealth, my *all*,
   I'll keep thy ftatutes, on thy name I'll call:
58 With fervent zeal thy favour I'll intreat,   115
   That thou thy promis'd mercy ne'er forget.
59 When on the conduct of my life I thought,
   My foul to rev'rence thy commands, I brought;
60 With fteady feet, without the leaft delay,
   Thy facred will I haften'd to obey.   120
61 The wicked pillage my domains, yet ne'er
   Thy law will I forfake thro' fervile fear.
62 To nobler heights I'll ftill my duty raife,
   And rife at midnight thy bleft name to praife;
63 And they alone fhall my affociates prove,   125
   Who keep thy precepts, and thy law who love.
64 Thou, who to man doft all his bleffings give,
   Grant that in this refolve I conftant live.

T E T H.

65 Firm to thy word, good God, with joy, with peace,
   Beneficent, thy fervant doft thou blefs.   130
66 O ftill, fince thy commandments I believe,
   A folid judgment and true knowledge give.
67 Before I was diftreft, I went aftray;
   But now I've fteadily purfued my way.
68 Thou'rt ever good-----beneficence is thine-----   135
   Direct me in the road to joys divine.
69 'Gainft me the villain-proud their flanders raife;
   But thee I'll faithful feek, and fervent praife.
70 While my delight is in thy law and thee,
   Their hearts are blinded with profperity.   140
71 Well was it then, that I diftrefs have known;
   Elfe I with them the fatal road had gone.
72 Thy law, thy ftatutes, to my foul appear,
   More precious far, than all the world holds dear.

J O D.

73 My frame, O God, created by thy hand,   145
   Grant me, thy perfect law to underftand;

My

74 My great protection thou, with heart fincere
   They'll joy to fee me, who thy word revere.

75 I know, O God, how juft thy judgments are;
   And that I juftly thy inflictions bear.   150

76 But now thy faithful promife call to mind,
   And let me folace in thy mercy find.

77 Yes; fince thy ftatutes make my fole employ,
   Let me thy bleft beneficence enjoy;

78 While perifh they, who with a caufelefs hate   155
   Purfue my foul, and to deftroy me, wait;

79 While thofe, who fear thee, and obey thy laws,
   In friendfhip join me, and affift my caufe;

80 While firm my feet the paths of duty trace,
   And dire confufion never fhrouds my face.   160

C A P H.

81 For thy falvation faints my foul; yet ftill
   I hope, and in that hope fweet folace feel:

82 Deny their wonted aid my languid eyes;
   Yet on thy word thy fervant ftill relies:

83 In expectation waftes my ftrength away;   165
   And yet I never from thy ftatutes ftray.

84 How long muft I this bitter anguifh know?
   When falls thy fearful vengeance on the foe?

85 For me the proud, who thy commands blafpheme,
   Dig deep the pit, and 'gainft thy fervant fcheme.   170

86 Juft are thy precepts, and thyfelf art juft;
   Therefore in thee 'gainft all their wiles I truft.

87 Me to the grave their wiles had well nigh brought;
   Thy law directed ftill my ev'ry thought.

88 O let thy mercy then my foul revive;   175
   So I thy law fhall conftant keep and live.

L A M E D.

89 For ever firm, O God, thy word remains;
   Firm as the heav'ns what once thy will ordains;

90 Thy faithfulnefs for ever is the fame;
   And lafts as long as earth's eftablifh'd frame: 180

91 What thou haft once determin'd ever ftands,
   For all things hear and wait thy high commands.

92 Unlefs thy ftatutes my delight had been,
   This bleft, this happy day, I 'ad never feen.

93 To them I owe my prefent profp'rous ftate;   185
   Therefore thy ftatutes never I'll forget.

94 Thine am I, gracious God;------thy fervant fave-----
   A ftrict regard to thy commands I have.

95 The wicked long have waited to deftroy,
   But ftill thy law fhall all my hours employ: 190

Thy

96 Thy law shall to eternity have pow'r,
  When earth, when time, when death itself's, no more.

M E M.

97 How does thy law my soul's affections sway,
  Thy law, my meditation all the day?
98 Thy bleſt commands, that conſtant with me dwell,   195
  Make me, that I mine enemies excel:
99 My mind by them illumin'd, high I ſoar,
  'Bove thoſe, who were my teachers heretofore.
100 Thro' them more wonders can I now deſcry
  Than all the ſages of antiquity.   200
101 Thro' them the paths to evil I've eſchew'd;
  Thro' them the road to happineſs purſued:
102 My great inſtructor thou, the road I trod,
  And ne'er forſook the ſtatutes of my God.
103 O how they furniſh me a ſweet repaſt,   205
  Sweeter than pureſt honey to the taſte!
104 By them the paths to error I decline;
  By them celeſtial wiſdom now is mine.

N U N.

105 Thy word directs me, that I never ſtray,
  A lamp to guide me in the perfect way.   210
106 I've ſworn (and what I've ſworn, I will obſerve)
  That from thy judgments I will never ſwerve.
107 Afflicted heavily, to thee I cry;
  O, mindful of thy word, ſwift aid ſupply.
108 The free-will off'ring of my mouth accept,   215
  And in thy ſtatutes thou my ſoul direct.
109 My ſoul unnumber'd perils ſtill ſurround;
  But on thy mercy all my hopes I found.
110 For me my impious foes have laid the ſnare;
  Yet from thy precepts I will ſcorn to err.   220
111 Them, as my ſole inheritance, I take;
  Them, I my ſole delight, my ſolace make.
112 Long as I live, my reſolution this;
  Thy law t' obſerve, to never act amiſs.

S A M E C H.

113 Vain-glorious thoughts my ſtrongeſt hatred move;   225
  And only on thy law I fix my love.
114 My ſhield art thou, my ſure, my ſtrong defence,
  Thy word, the guardian of my innocence.
115 From me depart; avaunt, ye impious croud;
  For I will keep the ſtatutes of my God.   230
116 And thou, my God, be ſtill my powerful friend,
  Nor let diſtracting ſhame my hopes attend.

117 The anchor of my hopes I'll not reject,
    Secure I stand, if thou my soul protect.
118 Destroy'd are all, thy statutes that desert,   235
    Their works are falshoods all; the tricks of art:
119 Like drofs, the impious doft thou sweep away;
    Soon are they gone; soon finishes their day.
120 Nay too, my trembling syftem quakes for fear;
    Left I the terrors of thy justice bear.   240

A I N.

121 In justice I've endeavour'd to excel;
    'Gainft me let not th' oppreffor's fchemes prevail.
122 With thy beneficence thy fervant aid,
    Left foes insulting fhou'd my peace invade.
123 Dim are my eyes with waiting for the hour,   245
    Wherein thou wilt exert thy healing pow'r.
124 I plead thy mercy-----let thy mercy fway;
    I only afk thy precepts to obey.
125 Myfelf thy fervant humbly I confefs;
    My proftrate foul with heav'nly wifdom blefs.   250
126 'Tis time, O Lord, that thou affert thy caufe;
    For lo! the wicked have made void thy laws:
127 While I of nobler price thy precepts deem,
    Than all the glitter grovelling fouls efteem:
128 Thy law I rev'rence, and thy name adore,   255
    And all falfe ways I utterly abhor.

P E.

129 Thy laws are wonderful, beyond compare;
    'Tis therefore they're the objects of my care.
130 His mind's enlighten'd, who thy word receives;
    Thy word bleft knowledge to the fimple gives.   260
131 Thy pow'rful word fo much my foul defir'd;
    My breath heav'd fhort, and almoft I expir'd.
132 All-gracious, view me with that eye benign,
    With which thou wonteft on the juft to fhine.
133 Me in my conduct by thy word fuftain,   265
    That no bafe paffion o'er my foul may reign.
134 From vile injurious pride preferve me free;
    So fhall I keep thy law, and reverence thee.
135 On me the glories of thy face difplay,
    And teach me to walk fteady in thy way.   270
136 Inceffant ftreams flow from my weeping eyes,
    'Caufe poor miftaken men thy law defpife.

T S A D E.

137 Impartial juftice, Lord, directs thy pow'r,
    Juftice divine the wicked fhall deplore:

                                   And

138 And all the laws thou'ft given us to obferve   275
    Teach us, that thou wilt ne'er from juftice fwerve.
139 What anguifh pains my foul, becaufe my foes
    Forget thy word, and thy commands oppofe ?
140 Yet purer ftill thy word than pureft gold ;
    Clofe to my heart thy word I therefore hold.   280
141 Poor tho' I am, tho' had in vileft fcorn,
    Yet from thy precepts I'll difdain to turn.
142 With killing griefs I ftruggle day and night ;
    Still in thy law I find fincere delight.
143 Thy facred law fhall time affault in vain ;   285
    When time's no more, thy juftice fhall remain ;
144 Thy juftice to eternity fhall live-----
    The pow'r to know thy will, dread father, give.

K O P H.

145 With faithful heart to thee, O God, I pray ;
    That I may never from thy ftatutes ftray.   290
146 Me with thy gracious mercy ftill protect ;
    And ne'er fhall I thy facred law reject.
147 E'er dawns the day, is this my conftant pray'r,
    And this my hope I faithfully declare :
148 When glooms the night, I thus thy pow'r intreat,   295
    And, wakeful, on thy law I meditate.
149 My voice, all-gracious God, benignly hear ;
    Give me, my life to govern by thy fear.
150 The impious croud that not on thee rely,
    That fport with mifchief, draw alas ! too nigh :   300
151 But nearer thou ; on thee will I depend ;
    Truth, equity, and judgment, thee attend.
152 Thy holy law, O God, I've known of old,
    Thy law that lafts, till time's laft hour is told.

R E S H.

153 My griefs confider, and thy fervant free ;   305
    Thy law I've not forgot ; but truft in thee.
154 Plead thou my caufe ; in fafety bid me live ;
    And, as thou'ft promis'd long, my foul revive.
155 Salvation to the wicked thou'lt deny ;
    Thy law they fcorn, nor on thy pow'r rely.   310
156 O let me long in peace enjoy the day ;
    Thy mercies, Lord, no numbers can difplay.
157 Many are they, that 'gainft my life combine ;
    Yet ne'er from thy commandments I decline.
158 I view'd the vile tranfgreffors with regret,   315
    'Caufe thy dread ftatutes they wou'd ftill reject.
159 O thou confider, how thy law I love,
    And to my faithful foul benignant prove.

T   True

160 True from the firſt thy word has ever been ;
　　True to eternal ages ſhall remain. . 　　　　　320
　　　　　　　·SCHIN.

161 With cauſeleſs hate proud tyrants have oppreſt ;
　　But on thy word my ſoul ſhall ever reſt.
162 Thy word to me more ſolid joy does yield,
　　Than e'en the richeſt plunder of the field.
163 Odious unto my ſoul baſe liars prove, 　　　　325
　　But thy bleſt law with ardency I love.
164 Seven times a day to thee my voice I raiſe ;
　　Seven times a day I celebrate thy praiſe:
165 What joys on all that love thy ſtatutes, wait ?
　　No heavy cares diſturb their happy ſtate. 　　330
166 For thy ſalvation long I've waited, Lord,
　　And therefore was I govern'd by thy word :
167 Obſervant of thy law I've conſtant prov'd ;
　　Thy ſacred precepts I've ſincerely lov'd ;
168 Obedience to thy will I've ever ſhewn----- 　　335
　　But thou my ſoul's moſt ſecret thoughts haſt known.
　　　　　　　T A U.

169 O hear me, gracious, when I thee addreſs ;
　　My ſoul, O God, with heav'nly wiſdom bleſs.
170 Let my complaint pervade thy pitying ear ;
　　With mercy, Lord, as thou haſt promis'd, hear. 　　340
171 Then, when thou'ſt made me perfect in thy ways,
　　My glowing lips ſhall utter all thy praiſe ;
172 My tongue the myſteries of thy word ſhall ſing,
　　For all thy laws from truth, from juſtice, ſpring.
173 On thy right hand ſecure let me repoſe, 　　　345
　　For I thy precepts for my guides have choſe.
174 To me thy laws ſincereſt joy afford,
　　And long I've waited thy ſalvation, Lord.
175 Still grant me life, that I thy praiſe may tell,
　　And in obedience of thy precepts dwell. 　　　350
176 Seek me, O God, as ſecks the ſwain his ſtray,
　　And never more I'll wander from my way.

P S A L M　CXX.

1　WHEN foes with cruel hate beſet me round,
　　　　My fame when impious tongues with ſlander wound,
　Quite deſtitute of aid, to thee I fly,
　To thee, dread father, and thou hear'ſt my cry.
2 O thou, who art to ſimple truth a friend, 　　　5
　And doſt the honeſt, guileleſs heart defend,

From ſland'rous lips and undermining tongues
Relieve my ſoul, and chaſe away her wrongs.
3 Ye villain-herd, who thus aſſault my fame,
Your tongues more fatal than devouring flame,
Who wound more deep with your invenom'd words,
Than pointed arrows, or than keeneſt ſwords;
What ſudden vengeance ſhall your ſouls await;
What dreadful judgments ſhall I deprecate?
5 Alas! the fatal miſeries I feel,
Amid the hoſtile croud conſtrain'd to dwell,
With men, who to humanity are loſt;
And all their cruelties for virtues boaſt!
6 For blood they thirſt, and wars and rapines pleaſe,
Nor have they joy in the delights of peace;
7 Fair peace they hate; from her embrace they fly;
War fills their thought, and furniſhes their joy.

P S A L M CXXI.

1 WHEN cruel foes with cauſeleſs malice arm,
. And ſtrike my haraſt ſoul with dread alarm,
Around the neighb'ring hills I'll caſt mine eye;
They haply may immediate aid ſupply. --
2 Yet ſure our God, of heav'n, of earth, dread Lord,
In my diſtreſs will quick relief afford;
3 Nor thou, my ſoul, be loſt in empty fear;
Thy God, to heal thy griefs, is ever near;
His eye, thy heav'nly guard, will never cloſe,
4 Nor aſks, like feeble mortals, ſoft repoſe.
5 Anigh thee, ſee, thy great preſerver ſtands,
And o'er thy head his ſhelt'ring wings expands;
6 By day he ſhades thee from the ſcorching ſun;
By night defends thee from the baleful moon:
7 At home thy ſure protector he'll be found;
In vain inſidious foes thy home ſurround;
Abroad he ſhields thee, or in peace or war;
He watches o'er thee with a father's care;
In ev'ry exigence thy life defends-----
Thy God's protecting mercy never ends.

P S A L M CXXII.

1 O BRIGHT, O glorious day! reſplendent morn!
With what a beamy luſtre doſt thou dawn?
What joy pervades my ſoul, the tribes to ſee
In pious throngs, dear *Salem*, viſit thee?

T 2

2 I too with them will croud thy facred gate ;   5
    To join the joyous tribes I carneſt wait ;
3 Yes ; thee I'll viſit-----thy bright domes ariſe
    In fair proportion, equal·with the ſkies :
    Fruitleſs th' attempt, in numbers to expreſs
    Thy lofty tow'rs and ſtately palaces.   10
4 Approach thy gates on this appointed day
    The faithful tribes, their ſtated vows to pay,
    Their annual rites t' obſerve ; in tuneful lays,
    In rapt'rous hymns, to ſing *Jehovah*'s praiſe.
5 In thee hath judgment fix'd her awful ſeat ;   15
    Thee has *Jeſſides* made his bleſt retreat ;
    From his high throne he hears the orphan's cauſe,
    Condemns oppreſſion, and ſupports the laws.
6 O favour'd city ! long may downy peace,
    May ev'ry joy, thy happy people bleſs !   20
    May heav'n it's choiceſt gifts on thee beſtow ;
    Around thy plains eternal plenty flow !
    May that dread pow'r, who long thy ſacred hill
    Hath choſe for his abode, protect thee ſtill.

P S A L M *CXXIII.*

1 O THOU, who haſt o'er all eternal ſway,
     Whoſe throne is heav'n, and whom the worlds obey ;
    When griefs diſtreſs, when foes around me riſe,
    To thy paternal love I lift mine eyes.
2 As with attentive eye the ſlave obſerves   5
    His maſter's beck, nor from his duty ſwerves ;
    As views the maid her miſtreſs' nod with care,
    That ſhe her favour and her love may ſhare ;
    So wait our eyes on our all-clement Lord,
    Till he his bleſt beneficence afford.   10
3 E'en now aſſiſt us, and our griefs remove ;
    Mere objects of reproach, of ſcorn, we prove ;
    Our foes inſult us, and our griefs deride,
    And utter their contempt with killing pride ;
    Our anguiſh'd ſouls their inſolence can't bear,-----   15
    Have mercy, Lord, and our confuſion ſpare.

P S A L M *CXXIV.*

1 OUR cauſe if heav'n's high king (may *Iſrael* ſay)
     Had not ſupported on that doubtful day ;
2 For us had he not fought, when haughty foes
    In all their wrath and all their fury roſe ;

                                                        When

3 When they fo thirfted for our guiltlefs blood, 5
  We ne'er their cruel frenzy had withftood.
4 Like fierce impetuous floods that break their mounds,
  And deluge with their fudden waves the grounds,
  On us they 'ad fall'n, and fwept us clean away,
  Our wives, our infants, and our lands, their prey. 10
6 But everlafting praife attend our God !
  From him our fafety in our danger flow'd :
7 By him deliver'd from their toils we are,
  As fcapes the fparrow from the fowler's fnare ;
8 On his ftrong arm we ftill depend for aid ; 15
  On his alone, who heav'n, who earth, hath made.

P S A L M *CXXV.*

1 ON great *Jehovah* who in faith rely,
   -Shall firmly ftand, like *Sion* feated high ;
In vain 'gainft *Sion*'s mount the winds arife ;
She braves their fury, and the ftorm defies.
2 As round *Jerufalem* the hills extend, 5
  And by their natural ftrength the town defend ;
  So guards his tribes *Jehovah* with his pow'r ;
  They never long his wanted aid deplore.
3 Long as his people to their God are true,
  Them fhall the impious nations ne'er fubdue, 10
  O'er them ne'er exercife defpotic fway,
  Nor lure their fouls from his dread laws to ftray.
4 To them, O Lord, who duly rev'rence thee,
  Whofe hearts are upright, fhew thy clemency ;
5 But all who deviate from thy facred law, 15
  Whofe fouls are finful, with thy judgments awe ;
  While bleft tranquility in *Salem* reigns,
  And peace and plenty crown her flow'ry plains.

P S A L M *CXXVI.*

1 WHEN God all-clement heard his people's cries,
   And freed them from their galling miferies ;
When he redeem'd them with his mighty hand,
And fafe-reftor'd them to their native land ;
'Twixt hope and fear diftracted, long they feem 5
Like men awaking from an irkfome dream ;
2 Then were their forrows into laughter turn'd ;
  They then rejoic'd as much as late they mourn'd ;
  Dried were their tears-----'twas all one fcene of joy ;
  While hymns of gratitude their tongues employ. 10

Nor lefs aftonifh'd at the great event
The *heathen* were, and murmur'd difcontent:
What wonders hath their God perform'd? they cry;
3 Wonders indeed! we therefore fhout for joy.
4 And thou our brethren, gracious God, reftore;　　15
In their hard bondage let them figh no more;
Let them return, and fill the crouded road;
As, when the fouth-wind blows, the rapid flood
Difdains confinement, and breaks down it's mounds,
And the whole plain in one wide deluge drowns.　　20
5 Who trufts his grain unto a barren foil,
Anxious he fears, 'twill not repay his toil;
But if glad rains a plenteous crop produce,
What fudden tranfports o'er his foul diffufe?
6 So we, from exile happily return'd,　　25
Where long our fetters and our woes we 'ad mourn'd;
Refeated in our native fields, are gay,
And our deliv'rer's clemency difplay;
Ourfelves to life, to liberty, reftor'd,
We, raptur'd, fing the mercies of our Lord.　　30

P S A L M *CXXVII.*

1 **T**HE great defign if not *Jehovah* blefs,
　　　Vainly we fcheme the lofty dome to ralfe;
Nor wakeful guards the city can fecure,
If not protected by Almighty pow'r.
2 If heav'n not man in all his toil fuftain,　　5
He rifes early to his work in vain,
In vain he to his reft does late repair,
And eat the bread of wearinefs and care.
But heav'n your friend, your fchemes have fure fuccefs,
Profp'rous your labours, and you fleep in peace.　　10
3 He fhow'rs eternal bleffings on your head;
Crowns with a num'rous race the genial bed;
With infant prate, diverting cares away,
Around your board the dear-lov'd ftriplings play.
4 And Oh! what nobler bleffings can afford　　15
To his lov'd fervants our indulgent Lord?
The warrior boafts not in the dufty field
So fure a buckler, nor fo firm a fhield.
5 Happy the man, whofe fons defend his life!
They're arms, that fail not in the day of ftrife;　　20
Afore the judge when cited to appear,
He'll not his wily adverfary fear.

P S A L M

P S A L M *CXXVIII.*

1 HE's trebly bleſt, who dreads th' omniſcient God,
    And in his perfect way with fear has trod.
2 Himſelf and his-----kind providence's care;
    The produce of his hands he long ſhall ſhare.
3 His wife, chaſte object of his faithful loves,
    Fills all his wiſhes, and his joys improves;
    Like beauteous olives in a fruitful ſoil,
    His children croud his board, and crown his toil.
4 Thus bleſt he lives-----his God will ſtill beſtow;
    Still from his God inceſſant bounties flow;
    And, more t' enhance his happineſs, he ſees
    His country bleſt with opulence and peace;
6 He ſees his own and country's welfare join'd,
    While fond parental tranſports fill his mind;
    He ſees his race of ev'ry good poſſeſt,
    Thanks his kind God, and dies ſupremely bleſt.

5

10

15

P S A L M *CXXIX.*

1 FULL oft (may *Iſrael* ſay) invet'rate foes,
    E'en from our infant-ſtate, have cauſeleſs roſe;
2 Full oft our peace, our lives, have they aſſail'd;
    But never yet their villain-ſchemes prevail'd:
3 Oft heavy burthens on our backs they've laid;
    And with their barb'rous cruelties diſmay'd.
4 But heav'n is ever juſt-----our bonds he broke,
    And freed his people from the galling yoke.
5 May ſure confuſion and vain hopes await
    The impious nations that our *Sion* hate:
6 Wither like graſs on lofty roofs, our foes;
    Like graſs that never to perfection grows;
7 Which, left the paſtime of the wanton wind,
    The mower ſcorns, nor will the gleaners bind:
8 Which views the trav'ller with a careleſs eye,
    Nor craves a bleſſing, as he paſſes by.

5

10

15

P S A L M CXXX.

1 SUNK in the depths of woe, to thee I cried,
    On thee, my God, in all my griefs relied;
2 " O hear me, Lord; attend my humble pray'r;
    " The ſad complainings of thy ſervant hear.
3 " If thou, vindictive, not our crimes forgive,
    " Ah! who can bear the dread award and live?

5

" But

4 " But ftill, our hearts to gratitude to move,
  " Thy dear, thy darling attribute is love.
5 " In thy fure word my only hope I place,
  " And wait the mercy of thy promis'd grace.   10
6 " As longs the watchman for the morning light,
  " Tir'd with the tedious duty of the night ;
  " My anguifh'd foul, o'erwhelm'd in mifery,
  " Afks for thy prefence, Lord, and burns for thee."
7 Hope in the Lord, ye juft ; his mercy ftill   15
  Redeems from woe, when we obey his will ;
8 From all her crimes the fpotted foul he'll clear,
  Difperfe each danger, and difpel each fear.

P S A L M CXXXI.

1 GOOD God, I am not infolent and high,
      Nor view inferiours with a lofty eye ;
  On wings of wild ambition I not foar,
  Nor things, too deep for human fkill, explore.
2 Humble and meek as is a new-wean'd child,   5
  Still my behaviour's affable and mild ;
  Not on myfelf I, arrogant, rely,
  But to the refuge of thy mercy fly.
3 And you, ye pious tribes, learn this from me ;
  The nobleft merit is humility ;   10
  Not on yourfelves, but on your God, depend,
  And he will ever, ever be your friend.

P S A L M CXXXII.

1 REMEMBER, Lord, the toils that *David* bore ;
      The woes for thee he fuffer'd heretofore ;
2 Remember too, how folemnly he vow'd,
  The facred oath he took to *Jacob's* God !
3 " My houfe (he faid) fhall not receive it's Lord ;   5
  " Reft to my wearied limbs fhall not afford
  " My downy bed ; fweet fleep fhall not furprize,
  " With all it's flatt'ring lures, my drowfy eyes ;
  " Till firft I know, a temple where to raife,
  " To his tremendous name, and fix the place."   10
6 This honour had I to my natal plains
  Defign'd ; but he, who o'er our actions reigns,
  Did to my duteous foul himfelf reveal
  The happy region, where he chofe to dwell.
7 Come then, ye tribes, with me your God attend,   15
  And in his temple 'fore his altar bend ;

                                                      And

8 And thou, eternal God, propitious, deign
  With thy bright prefence to illume the fane ;
9 Blefs there thy priefts in their devout employ,
  And let the pious foul exult with joy.   20
10 'If e'er thy *David* with a heart fincere
  To thee hath breath'd his unpolluted pray'r,
  E'en he, whom thou'ft adorn'd with regal fway;
  Receive the vows his off-fpring there fhall pay.
11 Oft haft thou folemn fworn, almighty Lord,   25
  (And time fhall ceafe ere thou forget thy word)
  " Thy progeny I'll on the throne maintain,
  " And they for ever o'er my tribes fhall reign ;
12 " If ftill thy children will my laws obey,
  " Nor from the perfect rule I give them, ftray ;   30
  " Their children fhall poffefs the regal pow'r,
  " Their children's children, e'en till time's no more.
13 " On *Sion*'s hill I've fix'd my own abode ;
14 " *Sion*'s the favour'd manfion of her God.
15 " With plenty her inhabitants I'll blefs,   35
  " And crown her fertile plains with rich increafe :
16 " I to her priefts will ev'ry grace impart,
  " And fill with folid joy each pious heart.
17 " From *David*'s loins a mighty chief fhall fpring,
  " Whom all the realms around fhall own their king ;   40
  " Whofe noble deeds fhall grace the royal line,
  " Whofe glorious light o'er all the earth fhall fbine :
18 " His enemies fhall view him with regret ;
  " While fhame and infamy their fouls await :
  " Long fhall he reign, and have a deathlefs name,   45
  " And everlafting time record his fame."

P S A L M *CXXXIII.*

1 THE mind fublimer pleafure ne'er receives,
    Nor earth a more delightful profpect gives,
Than when good men their faithful friendfhip prove
By cordial amity and mutual love.
2 'Tis like the oils, that, pour'd on *Aaron*'s head,   5
On his hoar beard their fragrant odours fhed ;
And to his flowing robe's extremeft hem,
Diffufing rich perfumes around him, ftream :
3 Or like the pearly dews the heav'ns diftil
On *Sion*'s mount, or *Hermon*'s flow'ry hill.   10
For where firm union reigns, celeftial peace,
With all her balmy fweets, their fouls will blefs ;

On

On them all bleſſings of this life attend,
And in ſincereſt joy their hours they ſpend.

P S A L M *CXXXIV.*

1 YE prieſts, by night that in his temple wait,
       The praiſes of your gracious God repeat; .
2 To him your hands in adoration raiſe,
   And mingle humble worſhip with your praiſe.
3 So he, yon ſtarry heav'ns, this earth who made,   5
   And ſhields his favour'd *Sion* with his aid,
   With eye benign your holy tranſports view,
   And all the bleſſings of his love beſtow.

P S A L M *CXXXV.*

1 ALL you, who in his ſacred courts attend,
       With humble awe who 'fore his altars bend,
   Sing, ſing the praiſes of the mighty God,
   And publiſh his tremendous acts abroad.
2 Yes; praiſe his mercy in ſublimeſt ſtrains;   5
   O'er the wide univerſe ſupreme he reigns;
   What nobler ſubject can the ſoul employ?
   What fill the heart with more exalted joy?
4 'Bove all the various nations that poſſeſs
   This ſpacious globe, his *Iſrael* does he bleſs;   10
   Our happy tribes have long his goodneſs known;
   Our tribes he made peculiarly his own.
5 Say, hath he not omnipotence diſplay'd?
   Can all the gods that human pride has made,
   That impious nations ſtupidly adore,   15
   With him compare in majeſty and pow'r?
6 Awful he wills-----lo! heav'ns and ſeas and lands
   Obey ſubmiſſive his ſupreme commands;
   His dread beheſt the deep obedient hears;
   The dark abyſs her maker's voice reveres.   20
7 He bids the vapours from the earth ariſe,
   And fills with genial rain the azure ſkies;
   His forky lightnings on the rain attend,
   And, rapid, in vaſt ſheets of flame deſcend;
   The winds are his; his mandate when they hear,   25
   They burſt their priſon-doors, and ſweep the air.
8 Thou, faithleſs *Egypt*, thou his wonders ſaw;
   He ſtruck thy *Pharaoh*'s harden'd heart with awe;
   Trembled thy chiefs when they at dawn beheld
   Their nobleſt herds and flocks beſtrew the field;   30
   And with what killing anguiſh did they ſigh
   To ſee their beſt-belov'd, their firſt-born die?

Great

10 Great nations by his arm did he fubdue ;
    He mighty kings with all their armies flew ;
11 Enormous *Og*, proud *Bafhan*'s plains who fway'd,   35
    Dread *Sihon*, whom the *Amorites* obey'd ;
    The haughty princes that in *Canaan* reign'd,
    And o'er her fertile plains fweet rule maintain'd :
12 Their lands to *Ifrael*'s faithful race he gave ;
    Their lands new mafters and new laws receive ;   40
    For ever ours, while we with holy fear
    The facred dictates of his will revere.
13 O mighty God, how glorious is thy name ?
    Eternal ages fhall thy pow'r proclaim ;
14 Juft art thou, Lord-----the humbled proud fhall own,   45
    Th' exalted poor, that truth fupports thy throne.
15 With thee compar'd, the heathen gods how vain ?
    What *bright*, what *glorious* deities they feign ?
    Poor imag'd *nothings*, form'd of fhining clay,
    To whom their ftupid vot'ries fruitlefs pray !   50
16 Mouths, true ! they have, yet have they not a voice ;
    Have eyes, yet cannot in the light rejoice ;
17 Their noftrils no rich fragrant odours tafte,
    Nor with the pow'rs of fpeech their tongues are bleft :
18 Bright objects of devotion's holy flame !   55
    And wife are they, fuch deities who frame !
    And wifer ftill, beyond defcription wife,
    The man, who on the god he makes, relies !
19 Ye happy tribes, from faithful *Abr'ham* fprung,
    Ye priefts, that to his hallow'd dome belong,   60
    And alfo all, who, ftruck with pious fear,
    With duteous hearts the fov'reign Lord revere,
21 Praife him, the God, on *Sion*'s facred hill,
    In *Salem*'s temple, who delights to dwell.

P S A L M *CXXXVI.*

1 IN joyous hymns and in fublimeft lays,
    The God of gods, the great *Jehovah* praife,
    The God, o'er mighty kings dread Lord alone,
    Who fuch ftupendous miracles has done :
    For great his mercy ; equal with his pow'r ;   5
    Lafts his beneficence, till time's no more.
5 'Twas he by his creating hand brought forth,
    From *nought*, yon worlds above, this fpacious earth ;
    This earth did for his fav'rice, man, provide,
    And bad the waters to their depths fubfide ;   10

Great

　　Great is his mercy, equal with his pow'r;
　　Lasts his beneficence, till time's no more.
7 'Twas he that fix'd the radiant lights on high,
　　With their bright blaze t' illume the azure sky;
　　That gave the sun to shed his beams by day,　　　　　15
　　The moon to bless the night with milder ray;
　　Great is his mercy, equal with his pow'r;
　　Lasts his beneficence, till time's no more.
10 When *Israel* in *Egyptian* bondage sigh'd,
　　By him the first-born of their tyrants died;　　　　20
　　He led his people from the faithless land,
　　By his strong arm and his Almighty hand:
　　Great is his mercy, equal with his pow'r;
　　Lasts his beneficence, till time's no more.
13 He bad the sea her turbid waves divide;　　　　　25
　　Her waves a rampier form'd on either side;
　　Safely we pass, and gain the welcome coast,
　　While *Pharaoh* and his threat'ning bands are lost;
　　Great is his mercy, equal with his pow'r;
　　Lasts his beneficence, till time's no more.　　　　30
16 Thro' the dry desart he his people led,
　　Slew mighty kings, and all their hosts dismay'd;
　　Great *Sihon* whom the *Amorites* obey'd,
　　And valiant *Og*, that *Bashan*'s warriors sway'd;
　　Great is his mercy, equal with his pow'r;　　　　35
　　Lasts his beneficence, till time's no more.
21 On *Israel* he their fruitful lands bestow'd,
　　That they might ever serve their gracious God:
　　And still, when in distress to him they cry,
　　Swift he redeems them from the enemy;　　　　40
　　Great is his mercy, equal with his pow'r;
　　Lasts his beneficence, till time's no more. •
25 On him depend the nations all for bread,
　　All by the bounty of his love are fed;
　　O'er heav'ns above, o'er earth beneath, he reigns;　　45
　　Praise all their maker in exalted strains;
　　For great his mercy, equal with his pow'r;
　　Lasts his beneficence, till time's no more.

P S A L M　*CXXXVII.*

1 WHILE in sad anguish, *Babylon*, we sat
　　　By thy *Euphrates*' stream, and mourn'd our fate,
Bewail'd our killing griefs, our galling chains,
And, fruitless, call'd to mind our natal plains,
Those plains, alas! we fear'd to see no more,　　　　5
What tongue can speak the cruel pangs we bore?

　　　　　　　　　　　　　　　　　Our

2 Our harps, that wont to tune our maker's praiſe,
 ⁼ That ſweetly anſwer'd to our joyous lays,
 ⁻Our idle harps, that long had been unſtrung,
 Then ſilent, on the mournful willows hung. ⸳ 10
3 'Twas then our tyrants thus their taunts expreſt;
 (E'en they who laid our glorious *Salem* waſte)
 " Now tune your voices to the heav'nly ſtrains
 " That us'd to glad your hearts on *Judah's* plains."
4 Shall *Babylon* our heav'nly anthems hear, 15
 The praiſes of our God, with impious ſneer ?
 Shall they with blaſphemy our ſongs deride,
 While thus we ſing to ſooth their barb'rous pride ?
5 O dear-lov'd *Salem*, if I thee forget,
 And that bright hill, where fix'd our God his ſeat ; 20
 If I not thee 'bove ev'ry good deſire,
 May then my hand forget to tune the lyre ;
 May fail my voice, when I, as wont, wou'd ſing
 My daily hymns to our Almighty king.
 Nor thou, *Jehovah*, thou forget the wrongs, ⸴ 25
 That fell from *Edom's* vile invenom'd tongues ;
 When with unbated malice they egg'd on
 The rageful foe to raze the ſacred town.
8 Thou too, O *Babylon*, thy fate ſhalt mourn,
 And ſure deſtruction waits thee in thy turn ; 30
 Happy is he, who in our cauſe ſhall riſe,
 And well repay thy horrid cruelties !
9 Happy, who, deaf unto the matron's moans,
 Shall daſh thy tender infants 'gainſt the ſtones !

P S A L M *CXXXVIII.*

1 DAUNTLESS, thy pow'r I'll ſing in nobleſt lays ;
 'Fore earth's proud tyrants thee, my God, I'll praiſe.
2 To thy bleſt temple I my eyes will turn,
 That hallow'd dome thy preſence does adorn ;
 Thy truth, thy mercy, and thy love proclaim, 5
 And celebrate in tuneful hymns thy name.
3 To thee I plain'd, and thou didſt hear my cry ;
 Didſt to my trembling ſoul due ſtrength ſupply.
4 Earth's ſceptred kings when they thy word ſhall hear,
 With humble rev'rence ſhail thy praiſe declare ; 10
5 Thy law ſhall own, thy mighty name adore,
 And ſing the awful glories of thy pow'r.
6 Tho' ſeated high on his etherial throne,
 Yet on the lowly looks *Jehovah* down ;
 And, while the proud diſdainful heart he ſcorns, 15
 The poor he loves, and, gracious, to him turns,

7 Me tho' a thoufand dangers fhou'd furround,
Tho' arm ten thoufand foes, my foul to wound ;
From him I fwift deliv'rance fhou'd receive,
And, free from peril, in his mercy live. ·   20
8 His great beneficence he 'as ever fhewn,   .
He, that will perfect what he 'as once begun ;
His humble fervant, faithful, he protects,
And ne'er the work of his own hand rejects.

P S A L M *CXXXIX.*

1 'FORE thee, O gracious God, I ftand confeft ;
Thou view'ft the inmoft fecrets of my breaft ;
2 Whate'er my heart conceives, my hands have done,
Howe'er from man conceal'd, to thee is known :
3 My night's repofe, the travail of my days,   5
Thy wifdom fearches, and thy eye furveys : '
4 Nor from my tongue drops one unheeded word,
But ftrait thou hear'ft it, O omnifcient Lord :
5 Whate'er I am, my frame, behind, before,
Is all the bright exertion of thy pow'r.   10
6 Such knowledge far tranfcends the narrow bounds
Of human lore, and all our pride confounds.
7 O how fhall I thy awful prefence fhun ? ·
To what dark corner from thy fpirit run ?
8 If I afcend to yon celeftial fphere,   15
Lo ! thou in dreadful majefty art there :
To hell's drear fhade if I direct my road,
E'en there I find the omniprefent God.
9 Me with her rofeate car if morn fupply,
And to the limits of the weft I fly ;   20
10 'Tis vain ; ftill in thy prefence I fhall ftand,
Expos'd to all the thunder of thy hand.
11 Say, fhall I hide me in the gloomy night ?
Alas ! thy prefence makes the darknefs light ;
Thy prefence drives the darknefs far away ;   25
With thee there's no alternate night and day.
13 Thou form'ft the clofe receffes of the mind,
And in thofe clofe receffes thee I find :
When a rude embryo in the womb I lay,
Thou gav'ft a cov'ring to my growing clay.   30
14 The perfect model of my frame difplays
Thy wond'rous wifdom, and extorts my praife ;
My mind runs o'er thy works with awe unfeign'd,
And owns the pow'r fhe cannot comprehend :
15 Owns, when at firft in fecret I was made,   35
Thine eye the gloomy dwelling did pervade ;
To

To forming nature was the certain guide,
And o'er the curious texture did preside.

16 Thou knew'st me, Lord, while yet my limbs were nought, 40
For in thy book my formless limbs were wrote;
And, 'fore they were, thy wonder-working mind
Their various pow'rs, their stated hours, design'd.

17 This when my soul revolves, in wild amaze
She's lost, and can but offer up her praise; 45
And vainly she attempts to number o'er
The dread stupendous wonders of thy pow'r:

18 For with much greater ease I'd count the sand
Which cast the flowing tides upon the strand,
E'en tho' I should eternal vigils keep,
And ne'er indulge my eyes in balmy sleep. 50

19 O when wilt thou the impious race destroy,
Whose thirst is blood, and *homicide* their joy;

20 Who with their villain-tongues thy works blaspheme,
And, wanton in their guilt, profane thy name?

21 Say, are not they the objects of my hate, 55
Who dare thy sacred statutes violate?
Count I not them among my enemies,
Who thee blaspheme, and thy dread pow'r despise?

22 Yes; sure I hate them, nor my friends shall be
The impious crouds, who dare dishonour thee? 60

23 O search, all-clement God, my honest mind;
Thou'lt still thy love my *ruling passion* find:

24 If with the wicked I thy laws contemn,
Consign me to eternal woes with *them*;
If with the righteous I thy laws obey,
Guide me with *them* to everlasting day. 65

P S A L M CXL.

1 PRESERVE me, Lord, from that insidious croud,
Those cruel foes, who've long my death pursued,

2 Who mischiefs 'gainst me constantly prepare,
Threaten my ruin, and denounce a war:

3 Whose tongues their deadly flanders scatter round, 5
And far more deeply than a viper wound:

4 Defend me from their villainous deceit,
And shield me from the violence they threat.

5 For my poor soul in ambuscade they lie,
And hope t' ensnare me by their treachery. 10

6 But thou, whom long my only strength I've made,
Hear, when I pray, and hasten to my aid;

7 My great salvation thou, my Lord, my God;
Oft hast thou aid in doubtful times bestow'd.

Now

8 Now too, make all their hopes, their counfels void,   15
  Their fouls infatuate, and confound their pride.
9 On their own heads fall all their killing wrongs;
  Wound their own fouls the arrows of their tongues:
10 From heav'n pour down thy dread confuming fire;
  Deep in th' avenging flame let them expire;   20
11 Drive falfe detractors from our earth away,
  And in their horrid fate thy pow'r difplay.
12 Thou wilt, I know, griev'd innocence fuftain:
  To thee the injur'd ne'er apply in vain.
13 Therefore the righteous in thy prefence dwell,   25
  Sing to thy name, and all thy praifes tell.

P S A L M   *CXLI.*

1 **T**O thee, all-clement God, I conftant cry;
    O hear me, and immediate aid fupply:
2 'Fore thee in pray'r when thy griev'd fervant falls,
  And on thy name with hands uplifted calls;
  Hear him, as when with incenfe he adores,   5
  And the pure off'ring on thy altar pours.
3 By thy dread fear be ftill my tongue reftrain'd,
  Guard clofe my lips, that I not thee offend:
4 Preferve me fteady in the perfect road,
  That I with finners ne'er blafpheme my God;   10
  Never with them in horrid guilt combine,
  But in their impious off'rings fcorn to join.
5 Me rather fmite the righteous and reprove;
  I'll count it all the kind refult of love;
  More welcome this, than when in flatt'ring guife,   15
  With foothing fpeech, deceitful men entice.
6 When fall the wicked from their high eftate,
  And mourn their fad viciffitude of fate;
  May they reflect, how friendly I advis'd,
  The wholefome warnings that they late defpis'd.   20
7 For me, thro' terror of impending death,
  Hang loofe my fhatter'd bones, and faint I breathe;
  My bones are fhatter'd like the tumbling oak,
  That mourns it's honours fall'n, it's branches broke.
8 But thou, almighty God, that rul'ft on high,   25
  Thou art my hope; I on thy aid rely:
9 Defend my life from each infidious fnare,
  From all the toils my cruel foes prepare:
10 Let me efcape, while I, enraptur'd, fee
  Thofe foes deftroy'd thro' their own perfidy.   30

P S A L M *CXLII.*

1 WITH ardent voice unto the Lord I cry :
 With uplift hands implore his clemency.
2 To him lay open all my secret grief,
 And in sad anguish beg his swift relief.
3 While in the depths of woe, O God, I lay, 5
 Thou know'ft how firm I trod the perfect way ;
 Thou know'ft how my inhuman foes prepar'd
 Their toils, thy faithful fervant to 've enfnar'd.
4 I look'd for aid, but no kind friend was near ;
 No friend, my faint and finking foul to chear ; 10
 No faithful friend to curb my cruel foes,
 To ftem the torrent, and their wrongs t' oppofe.
5 'Twas then, thy mercy I invok'd, O Lord,
 Call'd thee my refuge, and thy aid implor'd,
 Refolv'd, while life thou gav'ft me to enjoy, 15
 On thee and thy protection to rely.
6 O hear me now, for I'm in great diftrefs,
 With killing wrongs the men of blood opprefs.
7 From the drear prifon thou thy fervant raife,
 That he thy great, thy glorious name may praife ; 20
 That thee the righteous may in hymns extol ;
 The God whofe goodnefs guards the humble foul.

P S A L M *CXLIII.*

1 O SOV'REIGN Lord, my fuppliant plainings hear ;
 Give to my mournful plea a lift'ning ear ;
 Thy wonted faith, thy wonted juftice fhew,
 And fhield me, fave me, from th' obdurate foe.
2 Yet not my life too ftrictly thou furvey, 5
 Since none fo perfectly thy laws obey,
 None o'er their paffions hold fo firm command,
 As pure, as guiltlefs, in thy fight to ftand.
3 Lo ! my fierce enemy affaults my foul ;
 The victim of his villain-hate I fall. 10
 My difmal dwelling in the dark I have,
 Like them who long have moulder'd in the grave.
4 Therefore my foul was overwhelm'd with grief ;
 My heart well nigh defpair'd to afk relief :
5 Yet I remember'd ftill, (and ftill ador'd) 15
 That not in vain our anceftors implor'd
 Thy gracious mercy ; when thy pitying hand
 Difpell'd their dangers, and their fouls fuftain'd.
6 This gives me courage to fupport my fate ;
 With confidence thy mercy I intreat : 20

X

For thee I long, as long the thirſty plains,
Parch'd by the ſultry heat, for kindly rains.
7 Then hear, all-clement God ; ſwift aid impart,
Droops my afflicted ſoul, and fails my heart :
Shoud'ſt thou in anger turn thy face away,   25
Soon death wou'd drive me from the realms of day.
8 In thee alone I hope, on thee rely ;
With gracious ſpeed to my aſſiſtance fly ;
To thee my ſoul looks up, to only thee ;
Save her, my God, and give her liberty.   30
9 O ſhield her from the inſults of her foes,
For thee her fortreſs and her rock ſhe choſe.
10 Wiſe, good and juſt, art thou------direct my will,
That I thy ſtatutes ever may fulfil ;
That I no ear to error's lure may give,   35
But in the paths of duty ever live.
11 And that the grateful tribes thy name may praiſe,
Give me the bleſſings of my former days ;
And, that thy juſtice may to all appear,
Relieve me from this burthen of my fear.   40
12 Thy ſervant I------my griefs in mercy view,
And let thy vengeance my fell foes purſue ;
Deſtroy them, that they not diſtreſs me more,
And I'll that mercy gratefully adore.

P S A L M CXLIV.

1 O GRACIOUS God, thy glorious name be prais'd !
  'Tis thou that oft my drooping ſoul haſt rais'd ;
By thee inſpir'd, what wonders I've perform'd,
What armies routed, and what rampiers ſtorm'd ?
2 That life, that health, that manly vigour's mine, 5
That I with bright unſullied honours ſhine,
That oft I've triumph'd o'er the enemy,
And rule o'er mighty realms, I owe to thee.
3 O great Creator ! what is man, that thou
To him doſt ſuch continued favour ſhew,   10
Such wond'rous bleſſings doſt for him prepare,
And conſtant guard'ſt him with paternal care ?
4 What, but the empty pageant of a day,
That like a ſhadow, ſwiftly fleets away !
5 Bow down thy heav'ns, O mighty God ; deſcend ; 15
And let thy radiant guard their king attend ;
Let at thy preſence clouds of ſmoak ariſe,
From out th' aſtoniſh'd hills, and ſhade the ſkies.
6 Bid the vaſt *æther* with thy lightnings glow,
And with thy flaming arrows ſtrike the foe.   20

Stretch

7 Stretch forth thy aiding hand, and, gracious, save
From the drear horrors of the threat'ning grave
Thy faithful servant; lo! with impious rage
The villain-rout against my peace engage;

8 With words of death they arm their venom'd tongues, 25
And fill their cruel hands with fatal wrongs.

9 In hymns of joy I then my voice will raise,
And tune my lyre, to celebrate thy praise.

10 Thou hear'st the pleading monarch in distress,
And with deliv'rance doft thy *David* blefs; 30

11 Yes; with thy mighty hand propitious save
From the drear horrors of the threat'ning grave
Thy finking servant; lo! with impious rage
The villain-rout against my peace engage;
With words of death they arm their venom'd tongues, 35
And fill their cruel hands with fatal wrongs.

12 In strength, in vigour, may our youth improve,
As in a fruitful foil the laurel grove;
Lovely and blooming may our maids become,
Like polish'd columns of the stately dome. 40

13 May our rich fields a golden plenty yield;
May with their yellow sheayes our barns be fill'd;
And fast our flocks increase their fleecy breed,
That scarce our grassy plains their numbers feed.

14 Strong for his labour prove the sturdy steer, 45
While no shrill clarion strikes our hearts with fear;
While no fierce foe our peaceful cities threats,
No moaning, no complaining, fills our streets.

15 Bleft are the people, who without alloy
Such sweet felicities as these enjoy! 50
Yes; trebly bleft are they, whose God's the Lord,
The dread *Supreme*, by heav'n, by earth, ador'd!

P S A L M *CXLV.*

1 WHILE lafts this solid globe, my God, my king,
Thy name, thy pow'r, thy majesty, I'll sing;

2 Both night and day my grateful voice I'll raise,
And ev'ry hour shall hear me hymn thy praise.

3 Great art thou, Lord, and mighty is thy pow'r, 5
Too great for human wisdom to explore!

4 Yet, while yon starry lights above shall roll,
Thy mighty acts shall ev'ry age extol.

5 With me the varied nations all around
Thy majesty, thy glory, shall resound; 10
Old hoary age shall teach each list'ning son,
With pious joy, the wonders thou haft done;

X 2

7 With raptur'd hearts fhall hear th' aftonifh'd youth
Thy juftice, thy beneficence, thy truth :

8 How thou the wretched, gracious, doft relieve,   15
How flow to wrath, how ready to forgive ;

9 How good to all ; how all yon orbs above,
This earth beneath, thy gracious goodnefs prove,

10 Thy works, O God, and all thy faints fhall join
To hail thy glorious name in hymns divine ;   20

11 With Joyous tranfport their Creator fing,
The pow'r, the glory, of their heav'nly king ;

12 And to all ages and all nations fhew,
What to the ruler of the world they owe.

13 Eternal pow'r is thine ; fhall laft thy pow'r,   25
When dies the world, when time itfelf's no more.

14 Thou lift'ft the humble from their low diftrefs,
And giv'ft them affluence, and giv'ft them peace.

15 On thee all eyes are fix'd, nor fix'd in vain ;
Thy bounteous pow'r all nature does fuftain :   30

16 Thy hand thou open'ft, and on all below,
To their defire, unnumber'd bleffings flow.

17 Thy truth, O God, demands continued praife,
Juft in thy works, and holy in thy ways !

18 And they who to their God in faith apply,   35
Share ftrait thy goodnefs and thy clemency ;

19 And they, who to their God approach in fear,
Prove ftrait, all-clement, thou their fuit wilt hear.

20 Thou giv'ft them, ev'ry bleffing to enjoy,
And doft their impious enemies deftroy ;   40

21 Therefore with me all earth fhall fing thy praife,
Shall hymn thy pow'r in ever-grateful lays.

P S A L M *CXLVI.*

1 WHILE thou permit'ft me, Lord, the light t' enjoy,
Thy praifes fhall my grateful tongue employ ;
While o'er my limbs fhall flow life's purple ftream,
I'll make thy glory and thy pow'r my theme,

3 Confider all, how weak it is, how vain,   5
To truft in the moft potent fons of men,
Even in thofe, whom mighty realms obey,
Lords of the earth, exulting in their fway !

4 Lo ! foon their frail mortality they mourn ;
Soon to their parent *nothing* they return ;   10
And, when the icey hands of death affail,
Their deep-laid fchemes, their wily counfels, fail.

5 But bleft is he, who fteadily relies
On that great God who rules above the fkies ;

Who

Who fixes all his hopes on him alone,
Whom heav'n, whom earth, their great *Jehovah* own. 15

6 The heav'ns he made, the earth, the liquid main,
And all that heav'ns and earth and sea contain;
Firm is his truth, inviolate his word;
Ne'er from his gracious promise swerves the Lord. 20

7 When cruel tyrants humble souls oppress,
He hears their cry, and gives them swift redress;
He feeds the hungry, and the naked cloaths,
And on the captive liberty bestows.

8 The blind, the lame, from him soft pity find; 25
He gives the lame, to walk, to see, the blind:
The just, the righteous, his high favour prove,
The just, blest objects of his heav'nly love.

9 He the 'lorn widow and her babes befriends;
He the poor stranger in his path attends; 30
The guilty wretch he in his schemes appalls;
By his avenging thunder struck, he falls!

10 Therefore, while yon bright lamps illume the sky,
While yon gay sun his joyous light supply;
Our God on *Sion*'s sacred hill shall reign, 35
And o'er the nations endless rule maintain,

P S A L M CXLVII.

1 IN loftiest strains the great eternal praise;
Sing, sing his glory in sublimest lays;
What nobler subject can the soul employ?
Can charm her more?-----'tis ecstasy-----'tis joy!

2 Sure, *Salem*, thou wilt gladly sing the Lord, 5
Thee to thy wonted glory who restor'd,
Who freed thy captive-sons from galling chains,
And safely led them to their natal plains.

3 'Tis he that gives the anguish'd spirit ease,
Heals up our wounds, and sooths our souls to peace: 10

4 He numbers all the starry worlds above;
He gives them names, and at his will they move.

5 Great is his glory, infinite his pow'r;
And who his boundless wisdom can explore?

6 The meek are his, and he rewards their worth, 15
While feel the wicked his avenging wrath.

7 With grateful hearts the great *Jehovah* sing;
And tune his praises on the warbling string;

8 'Tis he the heav'ns with low'ring clouds obscures;
That on the plains sends down his fruitful show'rs; 20
That on the mountains bids his grass to grow,
And makes the barren hills with plenty flow:

The

9 The beſtial tribes that with their food ſupplies,
  And hears the callow raven, when he cries.
10 Not in the valiant chief, the man of might,   25
  Nor in the warrior-ſteed, he takes delight;
11 But in thoſe humble ſouls, ſincerely juſt,
  Who fear his name, and in his mercy truſt.
12 Thy mighty God, O happy *Salem*, praiſe;
  The tuneful voice, ye ſons of *Sion*, raiſe;   30
13 Your gates he binds with adamantine bars;
  He ev'ry bleſſing for your race prepares;
14 He crowns your cities and your plains with peace;
  And gives your yellow harveſts rich increaſe:
15 His awful voice our earth obedient hears,   35
  And with her plenteous gifts all nature chears;
16 His hoary froſts he ſcatters on the plains,
  And o'er the hills his ſnowy fleeces rains;
17 He binds the waters with his freezing air;
  His cold, ſay, feeble mortal, can'ſt thou bear?   40
18 He bids at will the milder winds to blow;
  The air grows warmer, and the waters flow:
19 On *Jacob* he his ſacred laws beſtow'd;
  His heav'nly ſtatutes to his *Iſrael* ſhew'd:
20 Not thus to other nations he hath done,   45
  Nor they his ſtatutes nor his laws have known.

P S A L M *CXLVIII.*

1 YE bright celeſtial choir, who live above,
    Who o'er the heav'nly plains at pleaſure rove;
Devoid of mortal crime, or grief, or care;
The praiſes of the eternal God declare.
2 And you, ye bleſt cherubick hoſts, that wait   5
More near around your great Creator's ſeat,
Ever prepar'd his mandate to obey,
In joyous hymns his boundleſs pow'r diſplay.
3 And thou, O ſun, who gild'ſt the day with light,
And thou, O moon, pale empreſs of the night;   10
And you, ye ſtars, with dimmer ray, that ſhine,
Sing forth his mighty name, his pow'r divine:
4 And you, ye various orbs, aloft that roll,
Scarce viſible to the enquiring ſoul;
And you, ye waters, far above that lie,   15
Beyond the regions of the azure ſky;
5 All, all, the glory of your God proclaim;
From his Almighty word your *being* came;
6 Your *being* ſtill his awful pow'r maintains,
And binds you faſt in adamantine chains;   20

Fix'd

Fix'd is your period, and you roll fecure,
From all th' affaults of time, till time's no more.

7 And thou, O parent-earth, that li'ft fupine,
And thou, O fea, do thou the concert join;
And you, ye monftrous tyrants of the main,   25
Which float exulting o'er her watery plain :

8 Ye fires, ye ratling hails, ye fleecy fnows,
Ye mifts, ye rains, each ftormy wind that blows;

9 Ye tow'ring hills, or you who gently rife,
Or you whofe lofty heights eclipfe the fkies;   30
Ye trees, or you whofe fruits the fields beftrew,
Or you, who, fterile, in the foreft grow;

10 Ye favage beftials, all that fhun the plain,
Or you, who love the neighbourhood of man;
Ye reptile tribes that humbly trail the ground,   35
Ye winged birds, that fkim the air around;

11 Ye various nations of the human race,
Howe'er diftinct in rank, difper'ft in place;
Or born to hold on earth imperial fway,
Or born fome lordly ruler to obey.   40

12 Howe'er diftinct in age, in fex, you are,
Or youths in prime of life, or maidens fair,
Or juft now trembling on the verge of life,
Or ftrangers yet to all it's cares and ftrife;

13 All, all, the praifes of your God proclaim,   45
All, give the honour due unto his name;
All, all, in heav'n, on earth, make him their theme,
All, own with grateful tongues, he's Lord fupreme.

14 And you, O *Ifrael*, from your mouths is due
Eternal praife, for much to him ye owe;   50
Peculiar objects of his boundlefs love,
Your thankful hearts in joyous anthems prove.

P S A L M *CXLIX.*

1 IN ftrains before unfung, in nobleft lays,
Ye faints of his, your great Creator praife.

2 Ye fons of *Ifrael*; 'tis to him you owe
Your life, your glory; grateful rapture fhew:
Ye blooming train, that round our *Sion* throng,   5
Sing to your heav'nly king a joyous fong;

3 Join in the dance in honour of his name;
With timbrels and with harps his praife proclaim.

4 All-clement, he his happy people loves,
And their religious melody approves;   10
And everlafting joy will he beftow
On all that humbly 'fore his altar bow.

Sing.

5 Sing then, ye faints, his glory all the day,
His mighty acts, his wond'rous works difplay;
And in the folemn filence of the night,   15
Ere laid to reft, *Jehovah*'s praife recite.

6 Your dread Creator's praife your bleft employ,
Let heav'n's high concave eccho with your joy;
While wield your nervous arms th' avenging fword
Againft the nations that reject his word.   20

7 Dread punifhments fhall then their fouls await;
They fly-----they fall-----perdition is their fate-----

8 Their fceptred kings, their haughty chieftains, mourn,
In hard, in ruthlefs chains, their fate forlorn;

9 And thus they feel from your victorious hand   25
The heavy woes your God had fore-ordain'd;
While thro' the regions of the world fhall fly,
Your bright renown, your glorious victory.

P S A L M CL.

1 LET great *Jehovah* animate our ftrains;
    To him yon fpacious firmament pertains;
High 'bove yon ftarry heav'ns he reigns fupreme;
Yon ftarry heav'ns his boundlefs pow'r proclaim.

2 His glorious deeds in tuneful numbers fing;   5
Difplay the majefty of heav'n's high king;

3 With it's fhrill clangor bid the trumpet join
The lute, the pfalt'ry, harmony divine!

4 With timbrels bid the virgins all advance,
To celebrate his glory in the dance;   10
While fprightly viols fweetly play around,
And folemn organs give a deeper found:

5 Let the fonorous cymbals fpeak his praife;
In concert, all, your grateful voices raife;
Yes, all that breathe this vital air, accord   15
With one confenting voice, to hymn the LORD.

T H E E N D.